The
FOODIE

WITHDRAWN

The FOODIE

Curiosities, Stories and Expert Tips from the Culinary World

JAMES STEEN

ICON

This edition published in the UK in 2015 by Icon Books Ltd.

Previously published in the UK in 2014 as *The Kitchen Magpie*
by Icon Books Ltd, Omnibus Business Centre,
39–41 North Road, London N7 9DP
email: info@iconbooks.com
www.iconbooks.com

Sold in the UK, Europe and Asia
by Faber & Faber Ltd, Bloomsbury House,
74–77 Great Russell Street,
London WC1B 3DA or their agents

Distributed in the UK, Europe and Asia
by TBS Ltd, TBS Distribution Centre, Colchester Road,
Frating Green, Colchester CO7 7DW

Distributed in Australia and New Zealand
by Allen & Unwin Pty Ltd,
PO Box 8500, 83 Alexander Street,
Crows Nest, NSW 2065

Distributed in South Africa by Jonathan Ball,
Office B4, The District, 41 Sir Lowry Road,
Woodstock 7925

Distributed in Canada by Publishers Group Canada,
76 Stafford Street, Unit 300,
Toronto, Ontario M6J 2S1

ISBN: 978-184831-988-2

Text copyright © 2014, 2015 James Steen

Typeset in Fournier by Marie Doherty

Printed and bound in the UK by
Clays Ltd, St Ives plc

In memory of my mum, the original Kitchen Magpie.

This book is for Louise, and for Charlie, Billy and Daisy,
with their ever-open beaks.
Let's eat in Prague!

CONTENTS

Introduction   1

1. The first aid kit   5

On burning or scalding the skin   5

On curing a headache (and jet lag and wrinkles)   5

On bee and wasp stings   6

On cuts to the hand   6

On curing a cold   6

On 'curing' the Black Death   7

On breaking a bone, or bones, in Parma   7

On the subject of bladder stones   8

The tansy: a must-have for the medicine box

     – and hey, you can make a pudding with it, too!   10

Paul Hollywood, what is the food of love?   11

2. The teapot   13

Who invented tea?   13

So what do we know for certain?   14

Tea: the wine connection   15

The arrival of clippers   17

A word about 'caddy'   18

Growing tea in England   18

Tregothnan Earl Grey Sorbet   19

How to stop a tea bore boring you   19

Ken Hom, what is the food of love?   20

3. The coffee machine   21

Johann Sebastian Bach's Coffee Cantata   21
Honoré de Balzac's day went like this   22
Coffee is for men because …   22
Drinking coffee   23
How to make Dublin Coffee James Joyce   23
The rise and fall of saloop   24
On the subject of baristas   26
Antonio Carluccio, what is the food of love?   27

4. The oven   29

On the Beeton track   29
The reign of Regulo   32
Roast beef with the oven off – how is that done?   33
The resting period   34
The trivet   35
The chef in the life of Florence Nightingale   36
The haggis: myths and legends   37
Pizza without the oven   39
A shoulder of lamb …   39
A leg of lamb …   40
The roasting of turkey   41
The 'juices running clear' myth   43
Marco Pierre White, what is the food of love?   43

5. The table   45

The Roman feast   45
Nap, map and kin   47
In posh restaurants   48
To be read out loud   49

To the manner born by Matthew Fort 50

The peculiar tale of the maitre d' who gave his life
    in pursuit of the perfect banquet 53

Lent when Lent was obeyed 54

Food, taste, and our palates 57

Meet the Poles: The Foodie's diary of feasting in Poland 58

6. The cutlery drawer **63**

The traveller who returned with the fork 63

7. The fridge and freezer **67**

Freaky fridge facts 67

What did we do before we had the fridge? 67

Ice cream comes to the streets 69

How to stop an ice cream bore 70

Famous last words 70

The cows of St James's 70

The cow that was milked the most (by an ad agency) 71

The cowboy's cow of Hollywood 72

Bacon's final experiment 73

8. The store cupboard **75**

Bovril: the soldier's sustenance 75

On matters concerning the salt pot and pepper mill 76

Ketchup 79

The hot dog by 'Hot' Doug Sohn 81

What on earth do astronauts eat? 83

Jason Atherton, what is the food of love? 84

9. The spice rack   85

The science of heat on the palate   85
Three recipes for Mauritian chutney   85
Dealing with spice bores   87
The mysterious curry cookbook   87
Francesco Mazzei, what is the food of love?   89

10. The toaster   91

The Grand Dame   91
Can toast be drunk?   92
Toast Day   92
Michel Roux, OBE, what is the food of love?   93

11. The fruit bowl   95

The Banana by Marcus Wareing   95
Which month, which orange?   98
On the subject of apple sauce   99
While sauce is on my mind...   100
How to stop a fruit bore   101
Five 'different' fruits to grow at home
   according to botanist James Wong   101
Why do the best raspberries come from Scotland?   102
Strawberries and cream   103
Pierre Koffmann, what is the food of love?   104

12. The locked larder   105

Turtle   105
Ortolan: the thumb-sized bird beneath the napkin   106
The most mind-blowing recipe   108
Frogs' legs? I always walk like this.   109
Do we eat horse? Neigh.   109

The delicate subject of foie gras, by James Martin   111
Michel Roux Junior, what is the food of love?   113

13. The wine rack and drinks trolley   115

Floydy and Blanc and the subject of cooking with wine   115
What makes Champagne bubbly?   116
From water to wine   117
The oldest wine cellar   118
The wine of prisoners   118
What to know about wine   119
What wines to drink from where   122
Passing the port   125
How to stop a whisky bore   125
The men behind the blends   126
Hangovers   126
The Amis novelists on hangovers   128
The Foodie's hangover cure: perchance the world's
    greatest remedy   130
Women and wine   130
Don't buy fake   131
Turning your home into a winery   131
The birth of AA   132

14. The vegetable rack   133

Salads of the 17th century   133
Dressing for a salad   134
The fashionable salad maker   135
On the subject of calories   136
A bit more about walnuts   137
Carrots and the battle to get us to eat them   138
The Smith recipe for a salad dressing   139

The potato   140
On garlic   141
On the prevention of tears when slicing onions   142
The perfect roast potatoes   143
Raw vegetables and the Hemingway diet   143
The veg pie that became carnivore's delight   144
Talking fennel with Mary Berry   144
Kai Chase, what is the food of love?   148

15. The fish kettle   149

The poaching of the wild salmon   149
Cock crabs and hen crabs at a glance   150
Jellied eels   150
Some tips about SHELLFISH and FISH   151
On the subject of prawns by Pascal Proyart   152
Antony Worrall Thompson, what is the food of love? 155

16. The egg basket   157

For the perfect poached egg   157
For the perfect fried egg   157
How Scottish are Scotch eggs?   159
Hungry soldiers   160
Do you like perfectly soft boiled eggs?   161
Ant eggs   161
Strange uses of egg timers   162
Adam Byatt, what is the food of love?   162

17. The cake tin   163

The king of cooks   163
Mary Berry's favourite cakes   164
The chocolate myth   164

The reluctant cook who wrote a bestseller 164
On buttermilk 165
Anton Mosimann, what is the food of love? 166

18. The window box **169**
Medieval herbs 169
A tribute to coriander 169
Coriander, cooking with it and the cure for colic
    by Manpreet Singh Ahuja 170
Does coriander reduce flatulence? 173
On finding snails in your window box 173
Marcellin Marc, what is the food of love? 176

19. The cocktail shaker **177**
The golden ratios 177
Let the good times roll 179
Sour 180
Berry sour 180
Collins 181

20. The truffle drawer **183**
On the subject of truffles 183
The Great English Truffle Correspondence,
    and the master forager Eli Collins 184
Truffle wisdom 188
José Pi\zarro, what is the food of love? 188

21. The (coco)nut bowl **189**
Worshipping the coconut by Manish Mehrotra 189
Dhruv Baker, what is the food of love? 192

22. The cheese board   193

Cheese gifts   193

Why can you eat mould in blue cheese and not on bread?   194

The world's most expensive cheese   194

Can cheese be frozen?   195

One of the smelliest cheeses   195

Eric Chavot, what is the food of love?   197

Epilogue   199

Acknowledgements   201

INTRODUCTION

Tie thy napkin!

'Never eat more than you can lift.'

—Miss Piggy

Foodies are unlike normal people.

They are obsessed with food and drink, to the point that nothing else really matters to them. They will pretend that other things are important, but, truth is, they are instantly aroused and distracted by the sensual pleasures of food, be it the whiff of a ripe Époisses, the fragrance of a tiny strawberry or the bashing of a meat mallet on veal.

When discussions arise concerning the subjects of politics or religion, foodies make good listeners. That is because they are immersed in thought, painting colourful layers of foodie-ness over the dull subjects: silently contemplating Abraham Lincoln's love of apples or how Pope Sixtus (*was it the fourth or fifth?*) drank not a sip, but a whole glass of wine in between mouthfuls of food.

Most foodies divide their attention between past, present and future, i.e. the last meal, the one that is currently being consumed and one that will be made or served soon.

Foodies are not discriminating. Foodies can be tall or small, young or old, or of medium height, medium build or middle-age. Anyone can be a foodie. Some people go through life with no interest in food. Then, one morning, they awake to discover a love of cooking, and they raise their hands to the heavens and say, "I was blind but now I can see the oven."

Come inside the mind of a foodie …

Imagine, God forbid, that an epidemic were to erupt on the Australian island state of Tasmania. World leaders and decent human beings would be concerned, naturally. Foodies, however, would also find a food association. They would dwell on the effect of the epidemic upon Tassie's sustenance enhancers, and they might ask themselves these questions:

What will happen to the Bruny Island Cheese Company and its heaving shelves of pongy Jack's Dad or soft, white Saint?
Will the crop at Tas-Saff (a farm of fine-quality saffron) be neglected?
How will the epidemic affect wine production of Jansz's sparkling wine (the vines thrive in the free-draining basalt soils in the Piper's River region)?

(Oh, by the way. Be sure to try Tasmania's pinot noir if ever it reaches your end of the table.) The point is, if a survey were conducted, nine out of ten foodies would admit to thinking *only* of food and drink; one out of ten foodies is a liar.

Foodies have existed since the beginning of time, but they did so without a name. The word 'foodie' was coined around 1980, when the world's population of foodies had yet to boom. In those days, foodies dreamt of prawn avocado, over-poached salmon and lumpy chocolate mousse. Today, the foodie still dreams of all those things.

This book began life in hardback form as *The Kitchen Magpie*. The magpie, incidentally, is a scavenger, looked upon with great favour by the Tudors because it kept the streets of the City free from filth. The bird is deemed 'unclean', but it is edible. McDonald's has yet to pluck it and pattie it, but in the late Middle Ages magpie beaks were all the rage. Worn around the neck, they prevented toothache, but that doesn't work anymore.

I want to thank you for finding the (valuable) time to read this slim but well-fed miscellany of morsels about food. Its content is inspired by the modern-day kitchen and the items that we take for granted as conveniences: oven, fridge, freezer, kettle, wine rack, even the fork. These accepted luxuries – and many more – provide the foundation of the chapters. The kitchen as we know it will not exist for much longer. Everything – fridge, cutlery, kettle, you name it – will be hidden from view within the next decade or so. The Foodie's quest is pleasure: to celebrate what is on sight today and, perhaps, tomorrow.

Speaking of kitchens, my career has taken me into scores of professional ones, not to cook but to interview great chefs and accomplished cooks on a variety of subjects. As part of the delightful process of compiling, collating and writing *The Foodie*, I have drawn upon thousands of hours of interviews, revisiting tapes, digital recordings and wine-stained shorthand notes. Food, every part of it, is best when shared. On that basis, I was driven to share what amounts to a feast of culinary knowledge, the food memories and the thoughts of Britain's best-loved characters in gastronomy.

For this book, I also asked a number of gastronomic idols and icons to answer one single question: *what is the food of love?* It is a question with no boundaries or limitations, and the responses, which are sprinkled throughout the chapters, are insightful and often surprising. These chefs and cooks, you see, opted not for so-called aphrodisiacs, but for the simplicity of comfort food – such as baked beans, roasted pigeon, and a ripe peach picked from the tree.

We can all play this game. My own food of love is ham and eggs, which my mother made when I was a child. One thick, sweet slice of honey-roasted ham beneath a fried egg, and there you have it: the contrast of runny, yellow yolk and firm, pink meat; the mix on the palate of hot egg and cold ham. Give me that humble dish for breakfast and my wife's shepherd's pie for lunch and the day is heading towards perfect.

Within these highly appetising pages you will also come across old recipes that have been forgotten. They have been gathering dust upon kitchen bookshelves and deserve to be remembered. I hope you agree. These recipes offer a swift, reassuring connection to all of our ancestors. You will read them, feel hungry, and will want to devour them straight from the page.

Though please do not eat this book yet.

1. THE FIRST AID KIT

....

Before embarking on the preparation of dishes, essential information for cooks regarding possible injuries and ill-health.

On burning or scalding the skin

Charles Francatelli, chef to Queen Victoria, suggests 'thoroughly bruising a potato and a raw onion into a pulp, by scraping or beating them with a rolling pin; mix this pulp with a good tablespoonful of salad oil, and apply it to the naked burn or scald; secure it on the part with a linen bandage.'

(Downside: this is terribly time consuming and painfully fiddly if the burn is on your hand.)

On curing a headache (and jet lag and wrinkles)

Don't reach for the aspirin: have a dozen cherries instead, especially if your headache is in British cherry season (between June and July). Cherries contain anthocyanins, which are also potent antioxidants to fight cancer. Sour cherries such as Morello contain significant amounts of melatonin, a hormone produced in the brain that slows the ageing process and fights insomnia and jet lag. It's also being studied as a potential treatment for cancer, depression and other diseases and disorders.

On bee and wasp stings

Do not bother searching for a dock leaf to rub on the sting. The search could take hours, or days. Instead, rub a wasp sting with vinegar. This will soothe, stop swelling and reduce pain. Apply bicarbonate of soda to a bee sting. Poppy leaves are also said to work for both.

On cuts to the hand

Scream. Then hold your hand(s) under cold running water for a couple of minutes. Then hold hand(s) above the head to reduce bleeding. Don't lose your temper with those who laugh at you for looking funny. This bit sounds odd, but it is better to be cut with a sharp knife than a blunt one, so keep your knives sharp. Sharpen a knife at 45 degrees with even pressure from tip to heel.

> **Knife tip**
> Always carry a knife pointing towards the floor.
> Unless lots of people are lying on the floor.

On curing a cold (Isabella Beeton, 1861)

'Put a large cupful of linseed, with ¼lb of sun raisins and 2oz of stick liquorice, into 2 quarts of soft water, and let it simmer over a slow fire till reduced to one quart; add to it ¼lb of pounded sugar-candy, a tablespoonful of old rum, and a tablespoonful of the best white-wine vinegar, or lemon juice. The rum and vinegar should be added as the decocotion [mixture] is taken; for, if they are put in at first, the whole soon becomes flat and less efficacious. The dose is half a pint, made warm, on going to bed; and a little may be taken whenever the cough is troublesome. The worst cold is generally cured by this remedy in two or three days; and, if taken in time, is considered infallible.'

On 'curing' the Black Death

In the highly unlikely event that you have an outbreak of this 14th-century pandemic in your kitchen, revert to the medieval cures. These include: avoid foods that go off, such as meat, fish and milk; take a live chicken, pluck it, and hold it next to the swelling; mix together roast egg shells (of a hen, if possible), marigolds and treacle and a pot of ale, heat over a fire, and drink twice daily; drink two pots of your own urine, one in the morning and the other before bed.

On breaking a bone, or bones, in Parma

First, a few words about the city of Parma in northern Italy. It is home to two of the country's most celebrated foods: Parma ham and Parmesan. Parmesan has been part of an astronaut's diet. Without gravity, the body's calcium levels drop and bones become weaker. Spacemen eat Parmesan because it is full of calcium and not affected by the environment, although it can spread its smell through the spaceship. We will come back to the food of space at a later point.

Meanwhile, authentic Parmesan must be stamped with the mark of *Parmigiano Reggiano*. If you try to pass off pretend Parmesan as real Parmesan then you will wake up with a horse's head on the pillow beside you.

When grating Parmesan cheese only very slight pressure should be exerted. Forgive my rusty Italian, but *la grattugia deve baciare il formaggio*, which (fingers crossed) translates as 'the cheese grater should kiss the cheese'. The point is, grating Parmesan should be a gentle action, not a bicep-building exercise.

But I promised you a tale of broken bones.

Sometimes when inhabitants of the region of Emilia Romagna break bones, they make pilgrimages to Parma's Parmesan dairies. It's an ancient custom. There, they will announce to the cheese-maker, '*Giuseppe, sono venuto per riparare le ossa rotte*' ('Giuseppe, I have come to mend my broken bones').

Assuming the cheese-maker's name is Giuseppe, the sufferer then plunges his cracked limbs into the basins of whey. Apparently, the Parmesan producers do not have a problem with this. Think I'm making this up? I'm not. Broken feet are first washed before plunging. Or are they?

NOTE: If Parmesan dairies are closed, head for A & E at the city hospital in Piazzale A Maestri.

On the subject of bladder stones

There is a connection between food, drink and bladder stones. Too much of the first and second eventually leads to the creation of the third, they say.

Bladder stones are mineral deposits which form in the bladder and disrupt the flow of urine. Try to pee and it's incredibly painful.

Sure, you can try to flush out the smaller stones by drinking lots of water but chances are you'll resort to one of three options of surgery: if my memory of surgery serves me well, a transurethal cystolitholapaxy, a percutaneous suprapubic cystolitholapaxy, or an open cystotomy. Correct me if I'm wrong.

That's a great deal of lengthy words but sufferers should be grateful that modern medicine offers these few options, plus heaps of anaesthetic. Consider for a moment the options that were available in the 17th century. There were two: either you existed in agony or endured an agonising operation.

Samuel Pepys, the great diarist who magnificently recorded his life between 1660 and 1669, was afflicted by a bladder stone, or even stones, in 1658. Gluttony may have caused it. Who knows? He underwent the operation, and one can hardly imagine the excruciating pain he endured, using only herbs, alcohol and perhaps opium for anaesthetic.

It is pertinent that, like the true gourmand he was, Pepys realised that the operation gave him an excuse to eat and drink even more. He would hold 'stone feasts'. These were annual tributes – well-oiled sessions with his mates – in remembrance of the stones and the success of the op. A bit like memorial services, but in a pub rather than a church, and with booze and food instead of prayers and hymns.

On Wednesday 26 March 1662, he records this diary entry about the stones and the commemorative meal: 'I had a pretty dinner for them, viz., a brace of stewed carps, six roasted chickens, and a jowl of salmon, hot, for the first course; a tansy and two neats' tongues, and cheese the second; and were very merry all the afternoon, talking and singing and piping upon the flageolet. In the evening they went with great pleasure away, and I with great content and my wife walked half an hour in the garden, and so home to supper and to bed.' *Went home for supper?* (By the way, flageolet is a small flute; Pepys never ate the flageolet bean, which was a French creation of a couple of centuries later, its name deriving from *fagiolo*, the Italian for 'bean'.)

A year later Pepys was on a mission to better the first event: 'Very merry at, before, and after dinner, and the more for that my dinner was great, and most neatly dressed by our own only maid. We had a fricasee of rabbits and chickens, a leg of mutton boiled, three carps in a dish, a great dish of a side of lamb, a dish of roasted pigeons, a dish of four lobsters, three tarts, a lamprey pie (a most rare pie), a dish of anchovies, good wine of several sorts, and all things mighty noble and to my great content.' Supper isn't mentioned.

The tansy: a must-have for the medicine box – and hey, you can make a pudding with it, too!

Samuel Pepys mentions that he had tansy. It is a plant, often common in meadows. It has yellow, button-like flowers and is also known as cow bitter and mugwort. It is bitter and slightly minty in taste.

Before it became a pudding it was a medicine. It was the Greeks who started using tansy for medicinal purposes and by the 10th century AD it was being used to treat intestinal worms, rheumatism, digestive problems, fevers, sores and measles. During the Middle Ages it was used to induce abortions. Then, just to confuse matters, it was eaten by women who wanted to conceive or prevent miscarriages.

In the 15th century, tansy was all the rage with Christians, who would serve it with Lenten meals to commemorate the bitter herbs eaten by the Israelites. Tansy was thought to have the added Lenten benefits of controlling flatulence brought on by days of eating fish and pulses, and of preventing the intestinal worms believed to be caused by eating fish. Tansy was a popular face wash (to purify the skin), a bathing solution (to cure joint pain) and was used to treat fevers, feverish colds and jaundice. You might have some growing in your garden. I have. Careful though, it can be toxic.

It was also used as an ingredient in the dish called tansy, which is like an omelette and can be savoury or sweet (made with apples or seasonal fruit). After several centuries, the herb fell out of culinary fashion and strangely was no longer an ingredient of the dish to which it gave its name. In his *Dictionary of Daily Wants*, published in 1859, Robert Kemp Philp offers the following recipe for apple tansy (containing no tansy):

> Peel, core and slice thinly four choice pippins. Fry them in butter.
>
> Then beat up four eggs, a teacupful of cream, twelve drops of rosewater, half a teaspoonful of nutmeg and a quarter of a pound of powdered loaf sugar.
>
> Pour this over the apples and fry the whole till brown. Garnish with lemon and strew with powdered sugar.

This looks very much like an apple omelette, and if you were to separate the eggs and then beat up just the yolks with the cream and sugar then this dish would be getting close to apples and our modern-day custard.

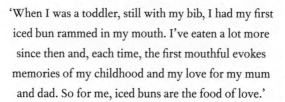

What is the food of love?

'When I was a toddler, still with my bib, I had my first iced bun rammed in my mouth. I've eaten a lot more since then and, each time, the first mouthful evokes memories of my childhood and my love for my mum and dad. So for me, iced buns are the food of love.'

—Paul Hollywood

2. THE TEAPOT

....

'Arthur blinked at the screens and felt he was missing
something important. Suddenly he realized what it was.
"Is there any tea on this spaceship?" he asked.'

—Douglas Adams,
The Hitchhiker's Guide to the Galaxy

Who invented tea?

In short, no one knows.

Granted, it's not a great start to a chapter. The myths of tea, however, are compelling so please don't skip this section.

It is said that in the 3rd century BC, a ruler of China called Shennong (aka Shen Nung) discovered tea when leaves burning on a twig beneath his cauldron were carried upwards by flames and landed in his vessel of boiling water. He tasted. He liked. There is also the story that the leaves fell from a tree into his cauldron. Again, he tasted and liked.

Both are neat and plausible stories, one of which may well be true. Before drawing a conclusion, though, consider other tales about Shennong. It is said that he spoke his first words within three days of being born, walked within a week and was ploughing fields at the age of three. Throw into the mix that he is also said to have been the inventor of the plough, perhaps when he was two, and that his body was transparent with the head of an ox.

He is credited with inventing the axe, the hoe, the Chinese calendar, acupuncture and agriculture ... and so the list goes on.

Shennong is a well-worshipped, mythical deity who introduced the Chinese to herbal medicine, tasting hundreds of herbs to test their medicinal qualities. He has various titles, including 'God of Five Grains' and 'Great Emperor of Medicine'. One day the poor chap tasted and died before he could swallow the antidote.

The tale of Shennong could be too much to swallow.

Then there is the alternative story of the Bodhidharma, the first patriarch of Zen, called Daruma by the Japanese. He sailed from India to China, went to Shaolin Temple and began a course of meditation that would last seven or nine years, depending on which barfly is telling the story. He was into year five, or was it six, when he momentarily nodded off. When he awoke he was so upset with himself that he sliced off his eyelids.

Pause.

Yes, he sliced off his eyelids so that he could meditate without falling asleep.

Where his eyelids fell, the compassionate deity Quan Yin caused tea plants to grow. Then Bodhidharma made some tea, and noticed that the brew prevented him from feeling tired. All who came after him drank tea as an aid on the path to enlightenment. Indeed, the Japanese characters for tea leaf and eyelid are the same.

A third story is more succinct. A Buddhist monk called Gan Lu (Sweet Dew) went to India, discovered tea, and brought it back to China.

Take your pick.

So what do we know for certain?

All tea comes from just one plant that is called *Camellia sinensis*. Though India has an indigenous tea plant, the *Camellia sinensis var. Assamica*, which comes from the Assam region of India and

THE FOODIE

gives us Assam tea, the original tea bushes planted by the British in Darjeeling were the native Chinese tea plants, the *Camellia sinensis var. sinensis.*

The different styles of tea (white, green, yellow, oolong, black) are a result of processing the leaves with different levels of oxidation. Meanwhile, Pu-Erh tea is a living, changing entity; due to microbial action it develops over decades to become mellower and sweeter. Pu-Erh can only be classified as Pu-Erh if it comes from Yunnan, from the broad leaf varietal of the tea plant, and it is sun dried.

Tea should be stored well in a sealed container. It is hygroscopic so will absorb perfume and humidity from the surrounding atmosphere.

Good water is important for making good tea. Ideally, it should come from the spring where the tea bushes grow. Admittedly, that could be a tough mission to accomplish.

Tea: the wine connection

Think of tea as being similar to wine. The role Buddhism has played in the history of tea in Asia parallels the role of Catholicism in the history of wine in Europe. Their respective beverages assumed ritual significance and those who were faithful to both traditions became devoted consumers.

For instance, Catholic monasteries became centres of grape-growing and wine-making. Similarly, Buddhist monks took up tea-growing and evolved increasingly sophisticated methods of tea manufacture.

Vinous innovations like champagne, invented by the monk Dom Perignon, had their parallels in China. Buddhist monks in China gradually developed the various types of white, green and oolong tea.

The quality of both tea and wine depend on climate and soil, or *terroir*. The drinks both need the skills of good producers, and both drinks contain tannins, which can be softened or mellowed. With wine we use a decanter. In the case of tea, pouring boiling water on the delicate, un-oxidised green and white tea leaves can dissolve the bitter tannins in the leaf. Brewing it cooler brings out the flavour without the astringency.

When sampling tea, slurp it with plenty of air, just like wine tasting: the characteristics of both can be experienced better around the tongue and palate. You can taste more flavour in the tea liquor when it is a bit cooler. Very hot and you cannot pick up all the nuances of the liquor.

Wine and tea have health benefits, unless you drink ten bottles of wine a day and take your tea with a kilo of sugar. The antioxidant properties of tea are the polyphenol compounds, which may well be effective against many diseases.

As with wine, tea can be incredibly expensive and valuable. Tea was so expensive when it was first introduced to Britain that only royalty and the aristocracy could afford it. It was locked in tea caddies to keep it secure from the servants. The caddy key was kept by the mistress of the house on a decorative chain called a chatelaine, which hung from her waistband. In the stately homes of the 18th century the mistress of the house would use the tea leaves first but they would then be infused again down through the pecking order of the servants, and eventually sold at the back door.

Moving forward a couple of centuries to 2002, a mere 20g (¾oz) of Da Hong Pao sold in China for about £20,000. This tea is particularly highly prized as it comes direct from the mother trees of this famous tea, not a clonal bush. The original trees are 350 years old. That's older than me and it's probably older than you.

The arrival of clippers

It was a challenge to get tea to the shores of Britain. Pirates were frequently on the lookout. The East India Company controlled the British trade in tea during the 18th century, and the company had its own currency.

It also ruled tracts of India with its own army. In the early 1800s ships were leaving England for China, laden with silver with which to buy tea, silk, spices and porcelain. This not only created a massive trade deficit but also made the ships attractive targets for piracy. The East India Company solved the problem of the trade deficit by growing highly profitable opium in India, which in turn was sold illegally into China in exchange for valuable merchandise – especially China tea for Britain. Hence, two opium wars.

So there was the issue of dodging the pirates, and also the chore of getting the tea back to London where demand was great. That's when tea clippers came along. These nippy vessels revolutionised ship design. They were built with a sleeker hull and greater sail area, which made them fast.

They could race the new season tea back to London faster than any other ship and pirates could never catch them. The clipper that arrived first won a prize and commanded the best price for the tea. Two tea clippers left Canton at the same time and, racing each other, they arrived at the London dock on the same tide 90 days later. Blue and white porcelain from China was used as ballast in the holds of tea clippers.

Perhaps the most famous clipper is the *Cutty Sark*, which can be visited in her dry dock at Greenwich in London. The ship's maiden voyage was on 16 February 1870, sailing from London and bound for Shanghai, carrying 'large amounts of wine, spirits and beer', according to the Captain's log. She reached her destination on 2 June 1870, and began the return trip three weeks later, laden with 1,450 tons of tea. She arrived back in London on 13 October 1870.

This was the first of eight voyages the ship successfully made to China in pursuit of tea, though the *Cutty Sark* never became the fastest ship on the tea trade.

A word about 'caddy'

Doubtless, the French would like to claim that the word caddy derives from the word *cadeau* (gift) because the tea-box is as ornamental as a gift. In truth, caddy comes from the Malaysian word *kati*, which was a measurement.

If you are in your kitchen and have tea leaves and scales to hand, measure out 604g (a pound and a third) of tea. There, in front of you, is a *kati* of tea.

In the 1800s, this weight of tea was put in pretty boxes and shipped back to Britain, where the *kati* was Anglicised and the box, rather than the measurement, became known as the caddy.

Growing tea in England

Tregothnan in Cornwall began supplying England's first and only tea in 2005. The current owner, the Honourable Evelyn Boscawen (the Boscawen family have lived on the estate since 1335), is the eighth great grandson of Earl Grey. But the Boscawens weren't the first people to consider the idea. Winston Churchill contemplated growing tea to fuel Britain through the war. However, the Prime Minister was told that the tea bushes would take five years to establish. The idea was abandoned and they stockpiled instead.

Tregothnan Earl Grey Sorbet

This is so refreshing and elegant and makes a lovely end to a dinner party, or a palate cleanser between courses. It's also surprisingly easy to make!

Ingredients:
30g (1oz) Tregothnan loose-leaf Earl Grey tea
300g (10oz) caster sugar
Juice of 1 lemon
1 litre (1¾ pints) of boiling water

Method:
Mix together the tea leaves, sugar and lemon juice in a large heatproof bowl and pour on the boiling water. Allow the ingredients to steep for at least 30 minutes, or longer for a more intense flavour.

Once cooled, pour the mixture into a freezer-proof container (old ice cream trays are perfect for this) and freeze for one hour. Remove from the freezer and mix the sorbet with a fork. Return to the freezer for an hour. Repeat this process a further two or three times, freezing then forking the mixture to ensure no large ice crystals can form. You're aiming for a fine texture, so the more you fork through the freezing mixture the better.

This sorbet is absolutely delicious served with tea-poached pears.

How to stop a tea bore boring you

When a tea bore is showing off, stop him swiftly by talking about bubble descriptions in China.

Traditionally, the Chinese can estimate the temperature of water from the bubbles as it heats.

First, tiny bubbles, which are called 'shrimp eyes' (75–80°C).

Then come 'crab eyes' (80–85°C).

These are followed by 'fish eyes' (85–90°C).

Then there is 'rope of pearls' – the first rolling bubbles (90–95°C).

This is followed by 'raging torrent' (95–100°C). This is nice and makes you want to poach an egg. But hang on because we're talking tea.

Last and certainly least there is 'old man water' (100°C) that has been boiled repeatedly and goes flat. Yuk!

What is the food of love?

'For me, it is the smell of Chinese sausages cooked in rice so that the fat permeates each grain giving it a rich flavour. It also evokes memories of warmth and comfort food at its very best. Since my mum made the dish for me, I have always regarded it as the food of love.'

—Ken Hom, author and TV presenter

3. THE COFFEE MACHINE

'Black as the devil, hot as hell, pure as an angel,
sweet as love.'

—Charles Maurice de Talleyrand, 19th-century
French diplomat, on how he liked his coffee.

If music be the food of love, and this chapter is about coffee, then let's croon along to …

Johann Sebastian Bach's Coffee Cantata

Written by Bach in the early 1730s, it's a comic one-act operetta about a strict father's efforts to deal with the coffee addiction of his daughter Liesgen. Here's an extract:

Liesgen:
Father, don't be so hard!
Then I would become so upset that I would be like a dried
up piece of roast goat.

Ah! how sweet coffee tastes!
Lovelier than a thousand kisses, smoother than muscatel
wine.
Coffee, I must have coffee, and if anyone wants to give me
a treat,
Ah! just give me some coffee!

Her father responds in song:
If you don't give up coffee,
You won't be going to any wedding
And you won't go out walking either.

Honoré de Balzac's day went like this

The 19th-century French novelist and playwright loved to, erm, play, but had a strict, self-imposed regime when it was time to work. Bed at 6pm. Wake up at midnight. Write for twelve-hour stretches, drinking coffee all the while.

He wrote: 'This coffee falls into your stomach, and straightway there is a general commotion. Ideas begin to move like the battalions of the Grand Army of the battlefield, and the battle takes place. Things remembered arrive at full gallop, ensuing to the wind. The light cavalry of comparisons deliver a magnificent deploying charge, the artillery of logic hurry up with their train and ammunition, the shafts of wit start up like sharpshooters. Similes arise, the paper is covered with ink; for the struggle commences and is concluded with torrents of black water, just as a battle with powder.'

Coffee is for men because ...

Napoleon Bonaparte drank it. He reckoned, 'Strong coffee and plenty, awakens me. It gives me warmth, an unusual force, a pain that is not without pleasure. I would rather suffer than be senseless.'

Benjamin Franklin, that wig-wearing, mucho-macho founding father of the US of A, drank it. He declared that among 'the numerous luxuries of the table ... coffee may be considered as one of the most valuable. It excites cheerfulness without intoxication, and the pleasing flow of spirits which it occasions, is never followed by sadness, languor or debility.'

Frederick the Great drank it. In fact, he had his coffee made with champagne instead of water. Hold on, that's not very manly. It's a bit girly. Red wine would have been more manly. Or vodka. But when Frederick was King of Prussia in the 18th century, coffee made with champagne was probably befitting of a warrior and master strategist of battles.

Drinking coffee

Coffee's flavour is at its best when drunk steaming hot, becoming increasingly bitter as it cools.

A dear but sadly departed friend, Terry Rowley, was in his youth a waiter at a posh hotel in London. Terry recalled serving Madame (Simone) Prunier, the elegant owner of Prunier, a well-known fish restaurant in St James's from the 1930s through to the 50s. He told me, 'Madame Prunier would order a pot of coffee which had to be boiling hot – and I mean as hot as possible! With it, she liked a glass of ice. She'd take an ice cube, drop it into the coffee and then drink it quickly.' The ice enabled her to get maximum flavour from the coffee without her lips, mouth and throat being scalded. Classy. Go one step further by heating the cups in the microwave before pouring in the coffee.

How to make Dublin Coffee James Joyce

From *The Alice B. Toklas Cook Book*, 1954

2 Jiggers Irish whiskey in a balloon wine glass
1 teaspoon sugar

Black coffee

1 Jigger Cream

Pour in black coffee, stir; as contents revolve add jigger cream slowly in circular motion. Allow cream to float on top of coffee. Do not stir again.

Excellent for after-dinner conversation.

FOODIE NOTE: Granted, this recipe appears to be Irish coffee prior to Irish coffee being christened Irish coffee. The Irish say they invented Irish coffee. The Irish-Americans claim it as their invention.

Whatever the case, Irish coffee seems to have been 'created' shortly after the Second World War. Whipped cream (instead of double cream) is considered an obscenity.

The novelist James Joyce (1882–1941) was a coffee drinker and a regular at Bewleys, the café in Grafton Street, Dublin, which he also mentions in *Dubliners*. And a jigger is what we know today as a measure or shot. The term stems from 'jiggermast', the small mast on a ship. The mast is little, as is the measure. It's between 25ml and 35ml, which is about five to seven teaspoons of liquid.

The rise and fall of saloop

The myths of coffee and tea, as well as the stories of Starbucks, Costa and all the other coffee shop empires, cannot be considered without a nod to the intriguing drink called saloop.

Sal what?

To anyone under the age of 200, saloop may mean nothing, but to anyone over the age of 200 it means a great deal. That's because it was the big-selling, much-adored skinny-latte-venti-with-flat-cap of the 17th and 18th centuries. Saloop was the poor man's coffee and tea; it was cheap while coffee and tea were expensive.

Coffee, tea and hot chocolate were the hot beverages that were introduced during the mid-17th century. These came from exotic climes – and exotic things, from pineapples to Chinese blue and white porcelain, were all the rage in Europe. Coffee was taken black and sweet, hot chocolate was enjoyed thickened with eggs as a nourishing breakfast.

And then there was saloop. It was made from salep, a flour that comes from grinding the dried roots of wild orchids. The salep powder was a thickener, and was mixed with water, sweetened with sugar and then flavoured, usually with rose water or orange flower. Milk was added and the drink was served hot and sold on street corners. You could have cinnamon sprinkled on it – Starbucks weren't the first.

Saloop came to us from Turkey and the Ottoman Empire at a time when we were obsessed with the Orient. The Turkish know the drink as salep, which is now more commonly made with milk rather than water, and flavoured with cinnamon. It's creamy, delicious and warming in winter.

So if you were rich then tea and coffee were part of your diet. For hoi polloi the drink was saloop. Say saloop out loud very quickly three times: saloop, saloop, saloop. It sounds like 'slurp' doesn't it? I'm convinced it's the origin of the word. I've no evidence, but slurp came into parlance at about the same time as saloop.

Apart from taste, saloop had other plus points. It was, for instance, considered to be an aphrodisiac. What wasn't? The Romans knew the orchid as satyrion, after the satyrs, the goat-like characters associated with fertility. The 15th-century Swiss-German physician, botanist, alchemist, astrologer and general occultist Aureolus Phillipus Theostratus Bombastus von

Hohenheim (aka Paracelsus) wrote: 'Behold the *Satyrion* root, is it not formed like the male privy parts? No one can deny this. Accordingly, magic discovered it and revealed that it can restore a man's virility and passion.'

Saloop was later made with the bark, roots and leaves of the American tree sassafras. In this incarnation, the drink is believed to purify blood. It is also claimed to be a blood thinner and used to reduce high blood pressure, eliminate toxins from the body, and sort out arthritis and rheumatic conditions. Add to the list its ability to fight colds and flu, bronchitis, gastrointestinal problems, kidney ailments and skin eruptions (including itching caused by psoriasis and poison ivy). It can be used to wean you off booze and fags. Is there nothing it can't do? Can it clean your car, pay your mortgage, beat up your bank manager? Yes, it probably can. Saloop is the clever clogs of gastronomic history.

It is also said that it is excellent for treating venereal disease. In America it was used by Indians and early settlers to treat syphilis.

The fascinating irony is that saloop's popularity went into freefall when people started to talk about its benefits for curing sexual diseases. 'Saloop, dear sire,' they would say to one another, 'is a good remedy for the pox.' That was the end of saloop. Drinking the stuff became almost shameful: if you drank it then it meant you were suffering from venereal disease.

People even stopped talking about it, which is why so few people have heard of it. Do you mind if we move on?

On the subject of baristas

The term barista, as in someone who makes coffee (and in particular a good espresso) is a new word in English. It's already recorded in the Macmillan English Dictionary and the latest edition of the *Longman Dictionary of Contemporary English*. Starbucks registered Barista as a brand name of espresso coffee makers in 1997. There is the World Barista Championship.

The word barista has developed from the same word in Italian, the gender-neutral term for 'barman'. There is evidence on the web for an alternative spelling, *barrista*, although this accounts for less than 10 per cent of occurrences. The usual plural is baristas, but in recognition of the Italian origin of the word, *baristi* is sometimes used, particularly by specialists in the coffee business.

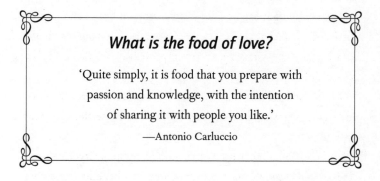

What is the food of love?

'Quite simply, it is food that you prepare with passion and knowledge, with the intention of sharing it with people you like.'

—Antonio Carluccio

4. THE OVEN

....

'Dine we must and we may as well dine elegantly
as well as wholesomely.'

—Isabella Beeton, 1861

On the Beeton track

Pour yourself a warming tipple (not too much, that'll do) and settle into the plumped-up cushions of a fireside armchair, to hear the enchanting story of a young lady called Bella. She lived a long, long time ago and spent her days and nights in the kitchen where she loved to cook for her Prince Charming, whose name was Sam, and their young children. 'I have always thought,' Bella would say, 'that there is no more fruitful source of family discontent than a housewife's badly-cooked dinners and untidy ways.'

Her selflessness was not confined to her own home. She gathered recipes and made a book of them so that, eventually, her acute wisdom, knowledge and blazing passion could be genuinely savoured in millions of kitchens by generations of cooks.

We know her more famously as Mrs Beeton, the editor of *Beeton's Book of Household Management*. It was published in 1861 but more than 150 years later many of the recipes remain the embodiment of all that is great in British cuisine. It is a classic in domestic and gastronomic literature, and the early editions (it was revamped beyond recognition in the 1900s) are an unequalled indulgence for anyone who lives to eat and cook. The first editions cost a couple of grand, too.

The legend of Mrs Beeton conjures up the image of a greying Victorian matriarch, an apron stretched across her sturdy frame, her Popeyed forearms covered in a dusting of flour; a rolling pin at the ready to wave at the grubby-faced grandchildren should they dare dip fingers into the cake mix.

Discard that image pronto. Isabella Beeton was, in fact, something of an angel who, like all good cooks, was a giver. She was just 28 years old when, in 1865, she succumbed to puerperal fever and died, four years after the publication of her book, and one week after giving birth to a son, Mayson.

True, the camera was not kind to her, but she was described as 'a very handsome young woman indeed, with heavy brown hair, a lovely erect carriage and a face whose beauty lay in its undeniable sweetness of expression … She had, too, charming little pianist's hands, neat and capable, that had already achieved a high proficiency on the pianoforte.' Born in 1836, the eldest of 21 children, she was 'a strong, small woman, full of go and energy and a fine organiser', which would help her compile that magnificent book.

Yet there would have been no Mrs had it not been for the Mr. Samuel Beeton was a man who liked to begin the day with 'a cold bath before a good breakfast'. He was a sort of frock-coated Simon Cowell: a publishing genius with the X factor. He published *The Englishwoman's Domestic Magazine*. New and exciting, the magazine catered to an untapped audience. It featured competitions and showed a thoughtfulness to the reader that made it significantly popular.

When Sam mounted a campaign to collect recipes 'from the Housewives of Great Britain' the readers responded by the sackload; these recipes were passed to Bella and provided the largest portion of the book. She was not, as is commonly thought, the creator of the recipes, though she claimed to have tested them all, probably refining them as she went.

At the Beetons' house in Pinner, in the London suburbs, Bella – along with her domestic cook and the kitchen maid – produced an astonishingly large variety of dishes. 'Nothing is to go into the book untried,' said Bella, thereby sentencing herself to the next three or four years at the stove.

The result – all half a million words of it – is nothing short of astounding. *Household Management* satisfies the cook, the gourmet and the historian. There are some thousands of entries, including hundreds of recipes under headings ranging from 'Soups' to 'The Common Hog', 'Bread and Cakes' and 'Invalid Cookery'. Mrs Beeton imparts advice about posh dinner parties and how to handle the servants: 'If they perceive that the mistress's conduct is regulated by high and correct principles, they will not fail to respect her.'

What emerges in Beeton's graceful style is her love of seasonal, local produce, and you realise that since the book's publication two world wars have obliterated all of her hard work. Never in our lifetimes has *Household Management* seemed more pertinent than now, and reprints (published by Wordsworth Editions) of the original are highly recommended and inexpensive.

Marcus Wareing, the Michelin-starred chef, is just as smitten. His menu at The Gilbert Scott at St Pancras railway station includes Mrs Beeton's Snow Eggs, which the French know as *Oeufs à la Neige* or *Iles Flottantes*. 'Her recipes are exciting and varied,' he says. 'She loved opulence and believed that "one of the chief considerations of life is, or ought to be, the food we eat". I agree.'

It was Bella Beeton who advised us 'a place for everything and everything in its place' and 'in cooking, clear as you go'. Hear, hear!

The reign of Regulo

For many years British home cooks used the term *Regulo*, as in 'bake for 10 minutes at Regulo 7'. Today, we'd say 'gas mark 7'. Or we'd say, 'Let's get a Chinese takeaway.' Yet what on earth does Regulo mean? Where did this oven setting originate?

The answer lies in a time between the two world wars. It was in 1927 that a new style of domestic oven was introduced to Britain, one that would delight the nation's home cooks. The 'New World Cooker' comprised a single oven, with a grill and gas hob. The advertisements bragged excitedly that this cooker cooked 'automatically'.

Six British firms had united to form one company, Radiation, which manufactured and sold these wondrous ovens. Rather than allow their customers to mess around with temperature readings in Celsius or Fahrenheit, the clever inventors simply put a knob on the oven with settings numbered 1, 2, 3, etc. These were the Regulo settings, Regulo being a trademark of Radiation.

So how did cooks know the heat of each setting? Simple. Radiation published the *Radiation Cookery Book*. Given away to customers, it contained hundreds of recipes, each recipe with its own Regulo gas mark settings.

As the cook, you merely followed the recipe; there was no need to think about temperature conversions. What's more, you could walk away from the oven while the food cooked. The book informed the cook, 'Watching, or attention, on the part of the user is not necessary. The same results can be repeated with certainty from day to day.' This was because 'the Regulo eliminates uncertainty from cooking'. All of a sudden cooking became regular.

By the late 1950s, 'Regulo gas mark' had become merely 'gas

mark', though the temperatures remained the same. The lowest setting of ¼ gives an oven temperature of 100°C, while gas mark 9 produces a scorching 250°C.

Roast beef with the oven off – how is that done?

You're reading the headline and saying, 'Roast beef with the oven off? Has the Foodie lost his marbles?' Either that or you're saying, 'Tomorrow morning I'm going back to Waterstones to ask for my money back.'

Hold on! This item is quite interesting.

A succulent rib of beef costs a small fortune, which is more than this book cost. However, a rib is without question a mighty and impressive cut to serve on a special occasion. Many cookbooks have devoted ample space to the subject of perfectly cooked rib of beef. Often the recipes are fancy and unnecessarily fiddly. Ignore them.

This recipe is intriguing (what's more, it works) because the oven is not on for the most part of the cooking process: something of a talking point when the beef is carved, served and relished at the table. This recipe originates from centuries past, when anyone who had an oven was the person you just had to know.

The most skilled networkers became friends with bakers. The baker, you see, toiled through the very early hours of the morning producing bread and pastries at high oven temperatures. When his work was done he shut down the oven but the residual heat remained high enough to cook 'slow' dishes such as casseroles and stews. If the baker was kind enough to put your rib of beef in his oven shortly before he shut it down then you would end up with a dish like this.

1. Preheat the oven to 225°C (440°F / Gas 7½)
2. Weigh the beef and rub salt and butter into it. Roast in the oven for six minutes per lb (450g).
3. Turn off the heat but leave the beef in the oven. Do not open the oven door. Leave it for two hours. Then you can open the door because then it is done.

The resting period

When meat is removed from the oven it requires a period of 'resting' before being carved or served. It's dull to talk about resting. But however dull resting might be, it does make meat taste better and is therefore a necessary requirement in cooking. In fact, the wise cook considers the resting period to be part of the cooking process.

There's a logic about resting. Let's start at the point at which the meat is in the oven. Heat approaches it from all sides and, in simple terms, the juices from the meat make their way to the centre of the meat. That bit is called *cooking*. When the meat is removed from the oven, the juices make their way back to the surface of the meat, creating succulence and a tender texture.

If the meat does not rest – or rather, it does not rest for long enough – then catastrophe! The juices will flow from the meat when it is cut. Tenderness will be lost. The meat will be dry and chewy. Your friends will decline all future lunch and dinner invitations. You will be pilloried. When you are walking down the street, people will point at you and say, 'There goes that person who serves dry meat.' If you are in Parma and break a bone and then go to a Parmesan dairy to get the bone fixed, the cheese-maker will say, 'Go away. You are the person who serves dry meat to your friends. Don't come here with your broken bone.' (Except he'll say it in Italian: 'Vattene. Tu sei la persona che serve carne secca ai tuoi amici. Non venire qui con l'osso rotto.')

How long should it rest? (The meat, that is, not the bone.) As long as possible. My friend Adam Byatt says, 'Rest meat for as long out of the oven as it spent cooking in the oven.' He also says, 'Rest birds and poultry on their back (breast side down) to retain moisture.' Adam and I have long conversations about the resting of meat. We really need to get out more.

Pork certainly benefits from a very long rest. The meat is as lazy as the beast from which it comes. If pork has been in the oven for two hours, wrap it loosely in tinfoil and allow it to rest for at least one hour. Other cuts of meat that have been roasted for two hours will be improved if they rest for 30–45 minutes. A cook's judgement is necessary; trial and error is worthwhile.

The trivet

Here's a tip: when roasting pork joints make a trivet of apples. Use apples such as Golden Delicious, which are floury and stop the meat sticking to the roasting tin; they colour slower than firmer apples and they will help to produce a flavoursome gravy.

Sounds great, you might say, but what the hell is a trivet? It derives from the Old English (or is it Old German?) 'three feet'. This refers to the tripod upon which a pot stood as the cooking took place in the hearth. The trivet raised the pot so that the heat could get under it. A trivet has subsequently taken on a different usage: it's the 'bits' that are placed under a joint of meat before it is roasted. It could be onions and other vegetables cut coarsely, in large pieces, or halved. It could be apples. The meat's juices run down on to the trivet and are absorbed. A tasty gravy is achieved.

When rolling out puff pastry always brush excess flour off before folding each layer otherwise the pastry won't stick together and will come apart in the oven.

When rolling pastry in a hot kitchen, first chill the surface with a roasting tray filled with ice for about 30 minutes before rolling out.

The chef in the life of Florence Nightingale

Alexis Soyer (1810–1858) was not merely a great chef. He was also an inventor with a mile-wide philanthropic streak. Soyer trained in the kitchens of Paris but he crossed the Channel to cook for nobility. At the Reform Club in London he opened amazingly modern kitchens with ovens that had adjustable temperatures and refrigerators cooled by water.

Frequently he cooked extravagant dinners for the wealthy and elite, but he worked tirelessly to help the poor and the needy.

During the potato famine he went to Ireland with the novel idea of 'soup kitchens' to feed the starving peasants. This man knew about nutrition. When he read the daily reports of the Crimean War, and of how soldiers were dying of malnutrition and food poisoning, Soyer volunteered to help. A sort of gastronomic superhero, he invented the 'Soyer's Field Stove', a cylindrical stove that the British Army continued to use for the next 120 years. He also helped Florence Nightingale look after the wounded; her nursing would not have been of use if the recovering soldiers were not properly nourished.

Indeed, Soyer's influence was so significant that the British Army realised the need for cooks in the regiments. And so the regimental cook came into being.

The haggis: myths and legends

In 2003 a survey of 1,000 American tourists visiting Scotland revealed that a third of them believed the haggis to be a small animal. About a quarter of those questioned were coming to Scotland to 'try to catch a haggis'. One American tourist described the haggis as 'a wild beast of the Highlands which only comes out at night'.

It is, in fact, a mixture of minced offal, oats, onions, spices and seasonings. These are all tidily contained, traditionally within a sheep's stomach, though nowadays within the intestine of ox or cow or in a plastic casing. Haggis is within the Marmite category, i.e. you either love it or hate it.

For those who love it, haggis is a hearty, peppery dish that adds much to the fried breakfast (though it can be used in many savoury dishes like shepherd's pie). Those who hate it may well agree with actor and comedian Mike Myers' comment that 'all Scottish cuisine is the result of a dare'.

Although haggis is Scotland's national dish it can be found in a variety of forms all over the world, where our predecessors worked out how to cook minced offal and grain within an animal's stomach or intestine.

The origins of the word are a subject of discussion. Similar dishes have developed in different countries, but the name 'haggis' probably derives from Scandinavia. The Swedish *hugga* and the Icelandic *hoggva*, mean to cut or chop, as you do when preparing the ingredients. The connections between Scotland and Scandinavia between the 9th and 15th centuries were especially strong, and it seems likely that haggis could have become established in Scotland during this period.

Or is it from the Germanic *haaken*, to hack? Or even from

the Old French *agace*, meaning 'magpie', because the haggis is an assortment of ingredients and magpies like assortments.

Let's see if we can find a recipe for haggis.

Venison haggis and fig tatin

(courtesy of the leading haggis makers, MacSween)

Serves 4

Use an oven-proof sauté pan or frying pan.

Ingredients:

1 roll all-butter puff pastry; 50g (2oz) unsalted butter; 50g (2oz) caster sugar; 8 fresh black figs; approx 230g (8oz) venison haggis, sliced; sea salt and black pepper to taste; 80g (3oz) onion marmalade; egg-wash (1 egg, whisked); fresh thyme, to garnish

Method:

1. Preheat the oven to 200°C (400°F/Gas 6).
2. Roll out the puff pastry and cut it to fit the pan. Set aside.
3. Gently heat a saucepan. Add the butter, sugar, and 2 tbsp cold water. Allow the sugar to dissolve. DO NOT SHAKE THE PAN!
4. Turn up the heat and cook to create a golden caramel. Watch the caramel as it thickens to ensure it doesn't burn. Cut the figs in half and arrange in the pan, flesh-side down. Arrange the slices of haggis evenly in the pan. Season with two pinches of salt.
5. Spread the puff pastry with onion marmalade. Place the pastry onion-side down over the top of the figs and haggis; press down the edges evenly inside the pan. Brush the pastry with the egg-wash.

6. Place the tart in the preheated oven to bake for about 20 minutes, or until the pastry is golden to your taste.
7. Remove from the oven and allow to stand for 3–4 minutes.
8. Place a large plate over the top of the pan and invert quickly to turn out the tatin.
9. Garnish with thyme leaves. Serve while hot.

Pizza without the oven

You want to treat yourself to home-made pizza but don't have a super-hot oven. Just use a frying pan instead. Heat on the hob a heavy-based, cast-iron frying pan until it is smoking hot. Meanwhile, pre-heat the grill to its highest setting. Roll out the dough and top with whatever topping you wish. Put the pizza on the upturned frying pan base and place under the grill. The combination of the top heat and the bottom heat together mimics a pizza oven better than any pizza stone in a domestic oven.

A shoulder of lamb …

… is best cooked slowly, on a low temperature.

Simply take the shoulder of lamb and score the fat with a dozen slashes – careful not to pierce the flesh.

Place it in a roasting tin, add a splash of olive oil to help it along, and then into an oven preheated to 190°C.

After 20 minutes turn the oven down to 160°C.

Every hour or so, pour a cup or two of warm water into the roasting tin.

Allow the whole shoulder to roast for about 4½ hours.

If you wish, place sliced vegetables and herbs such as carrot, parsley and onion into the tin in the last 90 minutes of cooking. To be even more adventurous, cook pearl barley in the tin – but be sure to top up with extra water for the barley to absorb.

A leg of lamb ...

... is best cooked fast, on a high temperature, as you can see from this recipe for Upside Down Hot Pot, which serves 4–6. It is so easy to make, and your home will be filled with comforting, uplifting cooking smells. Serve with lentils, a bottle or two of rustic red and an equally rustic loaf.

Ingredients:
280ml (10fl oz) red wine, maybe something from the south
 of France
4 large potatoes
500g (18oz) streaky bacon
50g (2oz) unsalted butter
500ml (18fl oz) water
1 lamb stock cube
1 × leg of lamb, approx 2kg (4lb 8oz)

Method:
1. Preheat the oven to 200°C (400°F/Gas 6).
2. In a saucepan, bring the red wine to the boil, count to 30, remove from the heat and place to one side. Peel and finely slice the potatoes (use a mandolin if you have one, but not essential). Using kitchen scissors, cut the bacon into diced cubes.
3. On the bottom of a large casserole dish place the butter and, with your clean fingers, rub it around the base of the dish. Wash your fingers.

4. Line the casserole with a layer of sliced potatoes; cover with cubes of bacon. Continue to arrange layers of potato and bacon, using up all the potatoes and bacon.
5. In a jug, make a mixture of the water, wine and stock cube (stock cube contains salt so don't season the dish until tasting at the end of cooking).
6. Pour the mixture over the potato-bacon layers so that it just covers the potatoes. If you need more liquid top up with water.
7. Place the leg of lamb on top of the potato mixture.
8. Place the casserole dish, uncovered, into the oven for 1 hour (30 minutes per kilo).
9. Remove from the oven and taste the sauce. If need be, add more salt.
10. Cover loosely with tinfoil and let the dish rest for 15–30 minutes. Serve in the centre of the table.

The roasting of turkey

Among the conversation topics of food lovers are the pronunciation of 'scones', and whether milk should be poured into the cup before or after the tea. (There is also the pronunciation of 'scallops', a matter of sincere interest to the outspoken personality Piers Morgan, who has just emailed me to say, 'Chefs say hard "a" as in "ballots", I prefer soft as in "b*ll*cks".' There is no 'correct' pronunciation of scallop, whose name derives from *escalope*, the Old French word for 'shell', in honour of the creature's stunning shell.)

Then there is the issue of cooking turkey. For one month of every year – December – there are intense debates and deep worries over the cooking of this bird.

Most of us do eat it at Christmas. Invariably, it is overcooked and dry. There are a number of reasons: it is too large for the oven so doesn't cook evenly; or the bird spends too long in the oven; or it isn't allowed to 'rest' for long enough. A combination of all of these is a guarantee of failure.

Turkey should be cooked quickly and allowed to rest in the time it takes to cook the accompaniments. I rest my turkey – about 5kg (11lb) – for two hours after removing it from the oven. It is only loosely wrapped in crumpled tinfoil. Does it go cold? No, it does not. Rest, rest, rest and rest – during which time the juices circulate within the bird, making it evenly moist and succulent.

Follow this method for perfect turkey. (Do NOT google 'cooking times for turkey'. The links will mostly advise you to cook it for too long.)

When choosing your turkey for roasting, allow 1lb (450g) per person.

Do NOT place tinfoil on turkey at the start of roasting. Use tinfoil before – and if – the bird begins to brown more than you would like. The foil might not be needed during cooking.

1. Weigh the turkey – it should be roasted for a total of 10 minutes per lb (450g).
2. Preheat oven to 190°C (375°F/Gas 5).
3. Place the turkey in preheated roasting tin. Coat the bird in one-fifth of a pack of unsalted butter.
4. Place in preheated oven.
5. After 20 minutes reduce heat to 180°C (350°F/Gas 4).
6. After a further 20 minutes pour one or two cups of warm water into base of roasting tray.
7. Allow the turkey to rest for at least 90 minutes in loosely wrapped, crumpled tinfoil.

The 'juices running clear' myth

Following on from the above item, we are frequently told to remove turkey from the oven when the meat is pierced with a skewer and the juices run clear. This is nonsense. Or rather, it is advice that does not make sense. If the juices run clear and the bird continues to cook – as it does once removed from the oven and during resting – then it follows that it will be overdone when it's time to carve. The juices should be ever so slightly pink at the stage of removing from the oven. That way the bird will be perfect after it has rested and when it is carved.

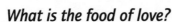

What is the food of love?

'When I was a little boy I went with my mother to Italy, to her home town. I remember sitting on a fence with my mother holding me. A man came along and gave us some green figs and my mother opened one with her hand and then gave it to me. It was my first taste of fig and I will never forget that its texture was more dominant than its flavour. It was runny with fig milk. I didn't like it. It's odd that the fig would become one of my favourite fruits.'

—Marco Pierre White, Britain's first chef, and
the world's youngest, to win three Michelin stars
(without ever having been to France).

5. THE TABLE

....

'The dinner is the happy end of the Briton's day.
We work harder than the other nations of the
earth. We do more, we live more in our time, than
Frenchmen or Germans. Every great man amongst
us likes his dinner, and takes to it kindly.'

—William Makepeace Thackeray (1811–1863)

The Roman feast

If the Romans brought the cherry to Britain (in the 1st century AD), who brought the cherry to Rome? It was Lucius Licinius Lucullus, great gourmet, gourmand and inspiration for the word *lucullan*, meaning 'lavish', 'luxurious', and 'gourmet'. He took the cherry from Persia, and also introduced the apricot to Rome. Among the various edible plants associated with Lucullus is a cultivar of the vegetable Swiss chard (*Beta vulgaris*); which is named 'Lucullus' in his honour.

He and his countrymen had inherited a tradition of fine food and fancy eating from their predecessors, the Etruscans. To emphasise the importance of earthly pleasures, a silver model of a skeleton or mummy was exhibited at their dinners – there as a reminder to enjoy the good things of this world while they could. Reclining on couches from about 2pm, they raised gold and silver goblets and toasted the genius of the Emperor.

They nibbled snails and liked anything cooked with ginger, coriander, mint and aniseed, or anise seed as they knew it. They loved olives, which they ate blindfold, trying to name the area where the olives had been grown. Olives were not cultivated in early Roman times, so were transported from North Africa and Spain in vast pots of honey, a fantastic preservative.

The first course generally included spicy sausages flavoured with Indian pepper, which had made an eleven-month voyage to Rome. There were dormice, which were stuffed with pork, herbs, pine nuts and more Indian pepper, and sewn up. They were baked by the trayload and then offered to the guests, who could then dip the dormice in honey and give them a coating of sesame seeds.

Syrian plums mixed with pomegranate seeds were brought from the Near East. Local vegetables were garnished with imported salt pickles from Byzantium. Oysters from Greece or Britain accompanied the first course. Live lions from North Africa and crocodiles from Egypt were paraded on chains around the aristocrats' table; sometimes the animals enjoyed a diet of petrified gladiators. Boar, roasted whole on a spit, was the star of the *cena*, or dinner (*cena* stemming from the Greek 'to cut', as you do at dinnertime).

The Romans had pans, pots and cauldrons. They had a frying pan, known as a *sartago*, which translates as 'mixture' (as in the medley of ingredients that were cooked in it). The sartago was also designed with a folding handle so that it could fit into kit carried by Roman soldiers.

The Romans used colanders, just as we use them today, for draining pasta and vegetables. They also used them to strain wine before it was consumed. If snow was available, it would be put in the colander and wine poured over it, thus giving a chilled glass of white. Delicious!

They used a weighing system that might sound familiar: *librae* (pounds), *unciae* (ounces) and *scripula*, or scruples – the latter were small pebbles that, in metric terms, equalled about two grammes. If you take a teaspoon of sugar in your espresso, then that's two scripuli.

Lucullus was an unrivalled gourmet. On one rare occasion he was eating alone and a meagre meal was placed before him. When he asked his slave why he was not given a feast, she replied, 'You do not have guests.'

'Nonsense,' he boomed in response. 'Lucullus is Lucullus' guest!'

Nap, map and kin

In the days of Roman feasts the table was covered with a sheet. This would serve two purposes. First, it stopped the table getting messy. Second, and more importantly, it gave the Romans something upon which to draw pictures of their travels and forthcoming journeys.

When they'd finished the meal they were left with a sheet of diagrams of mountains, rivers, roads and seas. They called this sheet of drawings a *map*.

By the time the French got their hands on the word, they called this table-sheet a *nape*. The sheet a cook wrapped around him or herself was christened a *naperon* – we know it as an apron.

The English already had their word: a tablecloth. But they needed a word to describe the little sheet that was used during eating, to dab the mouth and keep clothes clean. They couldn't call it a nape because that was large. So they added the suffix *-kin*, the Old English for 'little'. And they ended up with napkin.

In the professional kitchen we have the word *nap*. Chefs say 'nap the beef' or 'nap the fish', meaning to coat (or cover, as you would with a sheet) the food in a sauce.

In posh restaurants

In posh restaurants in France the waiter will open the meal by bringing to the table a petite dish and saying, *Voici un amuse-bouche*. In posh restaurants in Britain the waiter will bring to the table a little dish and say, 'Here is an amuse-bouche.' *Voici* is dropped in Britain because most of us don't speak French. However, 'amuse-bouche' is an acceptable phrase in certain circumstances. An amuse-bouche is, quite literally, something to *amuse* the *mouth*. A *mouth-amuser*, if you will.

This dish consists of just a few mouthfuls and is presented as a gift from the chef – it is an appetiser and serves to show off what is to come: the chef's creative talents. When chefs are bad they should never serve amuse-bouches. As they are bad chefs they are unaware that they should not serve amuse-bouches so they often serve them.

Of course, it is not a gift; it is not free. The cost finds its way on to the bill, hidden among the charges for starter, main course and dessert.

The term 'amuse-bouche' was born in Britain during the 'nouvelle cuisine period' of the 1970s, when chefs (French as well as British) served strange combinations of food on the same plate, e.g. roasted veal with macerated raspberries and fried banana. If the idea of roasted veal with macerated raspberries and fried banana makes you salivate, you could well have been a highly successful chef in the 70s and 80s. Or you could be an unsuccessful chef now.

In France, the proper term is *amuse-gueule* (*gueule* being a slang form of *mouth* and overly derogatory for posh restaurants). Whatever the case, the amuse-bouche is rapidly sliding out of fashion and may soon be banished to the kitchen dustbin by the back door where chefs smoke cigarettes and restaurant guests rarely go.

At the time of writing, the custom remains, but it's increasingly common for a waiter to serve the appetiser with the words 'Here's a little something from the chef'. Unless you happen to be in a Zulu restaurant, in which case the waiter will say, 'Nakhu a into kancane kusukela chef.' Or a Mongolian restaurant where the waiter will say, 'Энд тогооч-аас бага зэрэг ямар нэг зүйл байна.' A book is nothing if it doesn't test the editor and typesetter.

To be read out loud

Can you say *min-yoo*? Do you have the courage to say *min-yoo* aloud in a public place? Do you feel brave enough to say *min-yoo* on the tube, or if you are reading this in the United States of America, can you say *min-yoo* on the subway? Can you say *min-yoo* at a poker game, at a drinks party or in a restaurant? *Min-yoo, min-yoo, min-yoo.*

It sounds like a Chinese dish, doesn't it? Truth is, it takes us back to 16th-century England and a banquet at the stately home of the Duke of Brunswick. Picture yourself at the feast. Every now and again, as the magnificent dishes were being served, His Grace referred to a piece of paper in his hand. This piece of paper moved around: one moment it was on the table, the next it was in his pocket.

The guests were curious. What on earth was written on this piece of paper at which the Duke kept looking? He confessed. The paper was a list of the dishes that would be served that evening. The Duke, clearly a gourmet, knew what was coming next; he was ahead of the game, so to speak. The paper was a tiny note about the food. Tiny as in *minute*. My-newt.

'This is my minute,' said the Duke. Of course, when you say

minute – *my-newt* – in French, as the Duke would have done back in those days, it is pronounced *min-yoo*. The 't' is silent.

All it takes is one slight deviation over time and *min-yoo* becomes *men-yoo*.

To the manner born
by Matthew Fort

By way of introduction, Matthew Fort is one of Britain's finest food writers. For many years he was food editor of the Guardian. You may know him as the nattily dressed and masterfully eloquent judge on BBC1's Great British Menu.

Matthew has written two brilliant books about travelling around Italy on his Vespa, frequently eating long meals after which he sleeps on the roadside. Eats, sleeps and scooters. His most recent book is Sweet Honey, Bitter Lemons *but* Eat Up Italy *has the cheerful naivety of someone who hasn't a clue what he's doing.*

As Matthew has eaten in more restaurants than me, I politely asked him if he would write a piece for The Foodie *on the subject of manners at the restaurant table. Matthew is a man of such impeccable manners he said, 'Certainly.' So here, dear food-loving reader, is Matthew Fort.*

'Manners maketh man,' said William of Wykeham, Bishop of Winchester. The phrase became the motto of Winchester College and New College, Oxford. What utter tosh. Deception, skullduggery, pillage and worse have all been carried out under the veneer of good manners. Sir Harry Flashman is the patron saint of this particular kind of very English behaviour.

That is not to say that manners, good manners, don't have an important part to play in public conduct. In 1508 Baldassare Castiglione published *Il Cortegiano*, 'The Book of the Courtier', which set out in detail the essentials of good manners. However, it was Castiglione's contemporary, Giovanni della Casa, who laid down the precept 'Our manners are attractive when we regard others' pleasure and not our own delight' that lies at the basis of true good manners, and no more so than when it comes to eating.

We have moved on a bit since Erasmus wrote in 1526, 'You should wipe your spoon before passing it to a neighbour' and 'Do not blow your nose with the same hand that you use to hold the meat'. Whole volumes have been devoted to matters of table etiquette. 'The conventions of ordering food and of general behaviour are more or less the same no matter how elegant or simple the restaurant', declares *Debrett's Etiquette & Modern Manners* of 1981. In case you think the Debrett's model of manners is hopelessly dated, I should point out that it has a useful section on the etiquette of recreational drugs. And this in 1981.

The conventions of manners in restaurants in reality come down to the relationship between waiter and customer. Oh yes, there are the codices governing ordering wine, squabbling over who pays the bill, drunkenness, noise and so on, but these are minor matters compared to the rapport or otherwise between you and the person/persons attending to your every need. Now, waiters are the invisible people of the restaurant business; or they should be. You only really notice service if things go wrong. When all is going swimmingly right, you're carried away with that sense of easy luxury that you get from riding in the back of a Rolls-Royce. But if a waiter makes a mistake, you feel as if you're jolting over a dirt track in an old jalopy in which the springs have gone. This is where manners come in.

Treat your waiter as you would want to be treated yourself. Some customers have a problem in differentiating between service and servility, and treat waiters as serfs. Clicking your fingers, whistling, or shouting to attract attention are simply unacceptable and won't get you any better service. Next, show tolerance. Personally, I dislike being commanded to 'Enjoy' whenever a dish is placed in front of me. My natural bolshiness inclines me to respond 'No I won't', but I have learned not to moan about it.

And always feel free to complain. By and large, we British are hopeless complainers. We tend to grin and bear it and only cut loose with abuse when we've left the restaurant. It's too late by then. If you have a problem, diplomatic dialogue can usually sort things out. If things persist in going badly, there's no point in losing your temper. It's not going to improve matters. Summon the maitre d' and explain to him courteously what is going wrong. If he is any good at his job he or she will soothe your ruffled feelings, and turn you from a customer with a complaint into a regular.

Once I was leaving a restaurant when I bumped into the proprietor. In passing I observed that the fish was somewhat overcooked. The next moment I found myself pinned to the wall by my throat. 'What is the point of complaining now,' growled the proprietor, 'when you've eaten the evidence? Next time send it back.' Fair point, I thought. If there is an implicit contract between restaurant and customer, there is also one between customer and restaurant.

I know of one restaurant in which a lady was having lunch with a gentleman, not, I think, on the Castiglione model. The main had been served when the lady decided she needed to go to the loo. The waiter who showed her to the door was rather surprised to see the gentleman follow his lunch companion in. The waiter reported this to the suave, worldly maitre d'hotel. 'What should I do?' asked the waiter. Without hesitation, the maitre d' replied that the waiter had better divert other ladies to another loo elsewhere until the amorous couple decided to resume their lunch. In the meantime the main course was taken away. After 45 minutes, the couple reappeared, returned to their table, and lunch carried on as before. You see what I mean about manners making the man.

The peculiar tale of the maitre d' who gave his life in pursuit of the perfect banquet

Feasts are immense fun for those at the table, but this brief item is designed to make us all think of the poor people who organise the events and serve us.

François Vatel was the maitre d' who served in the household of Prince de Condé in Chantilly in the 17th century.

Vatel was renowned for his exceptional standards and need for perfection. Everything was going smoothly until that day in April 1671 when Louis XIV announced he would pay a three-day visit to the prince. Vatel would be responsible for overseeing the feeding of hundreds of VIP guests.

The king arrived on Thursday, and enjoyed a day of hunting. That bit was fine; there were no problems. However, things started to go dreadfully wrong (in Vatel's opinion) when there was not enough roast meat to serve the guests. Distraught, Vatel (who hadn't slept for twelve nights prior to the King's arrival), told a colleague, 'I have lost honour; here is an affront that I can't bear.'

The kindly prince went to Vatel's room to console him. 'Vatel, everything is fine: nothing was as beautiful as that dinner for the King.'

Vatel responded, 'My Lord, you are too kind. I know that there was no roast at two tables.'

'Not at all,' said the Prince. 'Don't fret about it, everything is fine.'

(By the way, I'm not making up this dialogue. It was well documented by guests.)

Next, the fireworks were a flop because it turned foggy. By now in a state of chronic despair, Vatel paced the floors while everyone else slept. He came across the fish supplier at four in the morning. The supplier had only two loads of fish. Vatel said to him, 'Is this all?' He was told, 'Yes.'

Vatel told another member of the household that he wouldn't survive this insult: 'my honour and reputation are at stake.' He went to his room, put his sword against the door and pushed his chest on to the blade. Look away now if you're squeamish, but he had to do this three times, as the first two attempts hadn't wounded him deeply enough to kill him.

And now for the twist. Alas, there had been a simple misunderstanding with the fish supplier. Shortly after Vatel's death the fish began to arrive by the wagonload.

Lent when Lent was obeyed

> Be merry, be merry, my wife has all;
> For women are shrews, both short and tall;
> 'Tis merry in hall, when beards wag all,
> And welcome merry shrove-tide,
> Be merry, be merry.
> —Justice Silence in *Henry IV, Part II*

You had to be sneaky to be a gourmand during medieval times. Fasting was frequent, gluttony was a sin and the church ordained that breaks from heavy food were needed on Wednesdays, Fridays and sometimes Saturdays. Fasting was seen as essential because the body was required to cleanse itself of the rich, heavy food of feasting.

You could eat while fasting but the choice was limited – a bit like a bad drinks party. Actually, at a bad drinks party you can't eat at all. You were supposed to avoid animal produce. So no meat, milk, cheese or eggs. Fish was allowable, as well as fruits, vegetables and breads.

Shrove Tuesday was a holiday devoted to feasting and merriment of every kind. Everyone ate pancakes, which were also known as flapjacks. Shrovetide was a season in its own right, and it was all about having fun. There was even a verb: to shrove, which meant to be merry. And people were said to be shroving when they were feasting and enjoying themselves.

The rules for Lent were quite confusing. Some areas of the Church abstained from all forms of meat and animal products, while others made exceptions for food like fish. For example, Pope St Gregory (d. 604), writing to St Augustine of Canterbury, issued the following rule: 'We abstain from flesh, meat, and from all things that come from flesh, as milk, cheese and eggs.' One rule allowed a person to have one meal a day, in the evening or at 3pm.

These Lenten fasting rules also evolved. Eventually, a smaller repast was allowed during the day to keep up one's strength from manual labour. Eating fish was allowed, and later eating meat was also allowed through the week except on Ash Wednesday and Good Friday. There were scambling or scrambling days: these were Mondays and Saturdays in Lent, when no regular meals were provided. Dispensations were given for eating dairy products if a pious work was performed, and eventually this rule was relaxed totally. (However, the abstinence from even dairy products led to the practice of blessing Easter eggs and eating pancakes on Shrove Tuesday, the day before Ash Wednesday.)

But in Britain there was a curious custom. A figure made up of straw and cast-off clothes was drawn or carried through the streets amid much noise and merriment, after which it was either burnt, shot at, or thrown down a chimney. This image was called a 'Jack-a-Lent', and apparently represented Judas Iscariot. Surely it was the inspiration for the model of Guy Fawkes that is wheeled around in a pram (a custom that seems to be disappearing).

Jack wore a headpiece made of a herring and Brussels' sprouts beside him. How do I know this stuff? Because Tudor minstrels would spring around, cheerfully singing the ballad called 'Lenton Stuff', which went like this:

> When Jacke a' Lent comes jostling in,
> With the headpiece of a herring,
> And say, repent you of your sin,
> For shame, sir, leave your swearing:
> And to Palm Sunday doeth he ride,
> With sprouts and herrings by his side,
> And makes an end of Lenton tide!

Of course, Lent brought headaches for butchers. During the reign of Elizabeth I, butchers were strictly ordered not to sell flesh meat in Lent. This was not for religious purposes but designed to diminish the consumption of meat during that period so that it was more plentiful during the rest of the year, and encouraged the fisheries and fishermen.

Butchers, however, who had an interest at court, frequently obtained a dispensation to kill a certain number of beasts a week during Lent, claiming that the meat was for invalids who could not subsist without animal food. Meanwhile, monks bred rabbits (which had been introduced by the Romans to northern Europe) for their tables. In *The Beast Within: Animals in the Middle Ages*, Joyce Salisbury writes: 'Monks favoured eating newly born or unborn rabbits for they were not considered meat and thus could be eaten on fast days.'

Over the years, modifications have been made to the Lenten observances, making our practices not only simple but also easy. Ash Wednesday still marks the beginning of Lent, which lasts for 40 days, not including Sundays. The present fasting and abstinence laws are simple: on Ash Wednesday and Good Friday, the faithful fast (having only one full meal a day and smaller snacks to keep up one's strength) and abstain from meat; on the other Fridays of Lent, the faithful abstain from meat.

Food, taste, and our palates

There are differences between individuals in the way we perceive foods. For example, for taste we have taste receptors in taste buds on the tongue, which are held in taste papillae. If we have more papillae, and therefore more receptors, then we can taste things at lower levels: 'supertasters' – the guys with more papillae on their tongues – have lower sensory thresholds.

There are, however, different types of taste receptor. So for bitter taste we have 24 different receptors; one of these is known to have genetic variants and there are certain bitter compounds that some cannot taste at all while others taste them as intensely bitter. This affects the way we perceive the bitter taste of brassica vegetables like broccoli and Brussels sprouts.

There are also genetic differences in our ability to detect certain odours, so some people cannot smell certain compounds at all.

Our taste cells are replenished every ten days or so. If this process slows down, for example with age, then our sense of taste can deteriorate to some extent. Similarly, damage to the odour receptors can affect sensitivity to odours. We are all born with an innate liking of sweet and savoury tastes and a dislike of bitter and sour, yet we learn to like bitter and sour tastes through repeated exposure to them. So just because you are more sensitive to bitter taste does not necessarily mean you will always dislike it.

Sometimes we hate something, e.g. beetroot, as a child and then love it later in life. This is due to learning to like over repeated exposures. Beetroot has an earthy flavour (geosmin) in it and we may become less sensitive to this with age, too. It's suggested that when we introduce food to our children we should persevere even if they reject it the first time. There's some truth in this: we need to learn to like, and the number of exposures required can be up to fifteen, but be careful not to have family battles that can lead to food aversions.

Meet the Poles: The Foodie's diary of feasting in Poland (as written for *Waitrose Food Illustrated*)

Day one

Daisy, four, chunders orange juice as we drive into Stansted Airport.

The minicab driver examines the mess and tuts. He doesn't know how much it will cost to have the back seat professionally cleaned. Repackaged and well marketed, his moaning and grumbling could be sold as a form of torture. He earns a ten-pound tip.

And so begins the family trip to Poland, to attend the marriage of Robert to Iza, who was a nanny to Daisy and her brothers, Charlie and Billy.

Iza faced a tough dilemma when Robert proposed: should she return to Poland to spend her life with her sweetheart; or stay with us, to be wound up daily by tantrums, fights, squabbles and food throwing (by the kids, that is)? Strangely, she went for the former option but sent us an invitation to the wedding to let us see that she was happy and had made the right choice.

We know nothing of Polish weddings, except that this one will last for the traditional two days, and that 150 guests will be there to toast the occasion. An additional clue has come in the form of a text message from Iza: 'Wedding plans going well. Had to make two car trips to collect vodka.' Louise and I think this means her car is small.

We fly into Lodz (pronounced Woodge) and are collected by Iza, who drives us for an hour to her home town of Rawa Mazowiecka. Her car is a massive hatchback, something akin to a Smirnoff delivery truck. We are staying in Robert's house, which happens to be in the garden of the house where Robert's delightful parents, Marek and Ewa, live.

Day two

I have rooted around Robert's house. His kitchen drawers and cupboards are filled with bottles of vodka, which satisfy his day-to-day consumption. Some bottles are empty, ready to be filled with the locally renowned vodka which is distilled by his father, Marek.

I make a pledge not to drink today, day one of the wedding.

There is a blessing at the home of Iza's mother. It is more of a get-together of the prospective in-laws, which include the bride's charming brother, Tomasz, and her personable uncle, Romek. The church service is conducted by a priest whose Polish renders him incomprehensible, so no different to many English-speaking clergymen.

Then to the ... well, I don't know what to call it. *Reception* is the wrong word.

The setting is a banquet room which is three times the size of the hotel it sits beside. A band plays Polish folk music. There are two tables, each long enough to seat 70 guests. At the end is the head table, for the bride and groom and their immediate families.

The tables are laden with food, abundance like you have never seen at a modern-day wedding in Britain. It is almost Edwardian in extravagance. Pretty much every square inch of tablecloth is covered with something to eat (sweet and savoury) or drink (non-alcoholic or alcoholic).

There are five-tiered cake stands holding coconut sponge and vanilla cream, or chocolate sponge and coffee cream, or pastries filled, let's say, with fruit purée and pastry cream, along with gingerbread and doughnuts.

There are salads of sliced beetroot, grated carrot and dill pickle. There are wide-brimmed, shallow bowls of fish, be it herring, eel or pike, in aspic jelly. There are dishes of roast pork with a prune stuffing, as well as *bigos*, the national dish made from cabbage and mushrooms.

In one corner of the room, there is something that looks like a market stall, colourfully decorated and eye-catching. It is a carnivore's feast, the home to hams, tongue and *wiejska kiszka* (black pudding): products of the pig, from snout to tail.

We take our seats (there is no seating plan) and I notice that for every six guests there is only one bottle of red wine, and it is Bull's Blood, as drunk by fire-eaters. In fact, the wine (alongside water and fizzy drinks) is not really there to be drunk. Instead, the guests drink vodka and now, as I look along the tables, it becomes clear why Iza had to do the two trips.

There are scores of bottles of Pan Tadeusz, the popular Polish vodka (and named after the national epos written by Adam Mickiewicz). It is 80 proof and is being consumed swiftly and with enthusiasm. All around me, guests are demolishing the stuff, shot after shot.

More high-protein, high-calorie food is served to each guest by waiters in white uniforms. First, a clear, nutritious broth of chicken and fine noodles; then chicken escalope cooked in breadcrumbs; lemon tea arrives, perhaps as a palate-cleanser; next comes steak *tartare* with its garnish of chopped onions and pickles.

Somewhere in between I am cornered by brother Tomasz and Uncle Romek and dragged off to taste from a barrel of vodka. 'I'm not drinking,' doesn't work as an excuse. We do a shot. They tell me that vodka leaves you with a clear head the following morning. We do another shot. Then another.

They do not talk English and I do not talk Polish but we seem to have 'conversations' about Marlboro cigarettes, and the benefits of adding water to whisky. More guests join in the debates. We talk intensely about speed cameras (*fotoradas*), or at least that's what I was talking about.

Every now and again I feel a tug at my elbow and then – whoosh – I am whisked off to the dance floor and spun around (shaken and stirred), more often than not by Iza's wild-eyed godmother. We do the conga. Then we stamp our feet and jump up and down. The band is playing a song, the lyrics of which translate roughly as: 'Drink the vodka or you will die.' I oblige …

Day three
I awake at 4am. Have I died? I climb out of bed, climb out of my suit, and climb back into bed.

Three hours later I am standing under a cold shower, numbed by the previous night. An hour after that, I am still standing under the cold shower, numbed by the previous night and by the cold water. Louise fills in the blanks: I was helped from the party and poured into a car by Tomasz and Uncle Romek. Then Louise, sober, drove the Steens home.

We go back to the same venue for day two of the wedding. The party has the same band and much of the same food, save for *borsch*, the rich beetroot soup. But the crowd has lost a third of its number to alcohol poisoning. I stick to lemonade. Brother Tomasz and Uncle Romek stick to vodka. 'Romek,' I say, 'You look like you slept in your car.'

'Yes,' he says and wanders off. Tomasz tells me that Uncle Romek slept in his car.

Guests say I have proved myself as a man because last night I drank Uncle Romek under the table. This is wrong. I did not drink him under the table; he helped me to leave. But no one except Louise remembers that.

Day four

Return to London. Just as we are about to show our passports at passport control, Daisy has a fight with Billy, six. Billy the Kid runs off, departing through Arrivals. It takes ten minutes to find him and enter the country.

We are collected by the driver in whose minicab Daisy chundered. He drops us at home and then hands me a receipt for twenty pounds – the cost, he says, for the car's back seat to be professionally cleaned.

A final thought: in the old days Polish weddings often lasted a week.

6. THE CUTLERY DRAWER

....

'Dig it man! There goes Mack the Knife.'

—Louis Armstrong, 'Mack the Knife'

The traveller who returned with the fork (includes one reference to naked breasts)

Forks came into being in the 14th century but were a luxury enjoyed by only the ridiculously rich. Royalty and nobility would use them for eating honeyed fruits and sweetmeats so as not to make their blue-blooded hands sticky.

Quick digression: why are sweetmeats called sweetmeats when they don't contain meat? It is because *mete* is the Old English word for food.

But it was not until the 1600s that the fork earned star status, becoming popular on the tables of Britain. The Elizabethans had one Thomas Coryat to thank for that. Born in Somerset, Coryat was a traveller and writer whose catchy-titled tomes included *Coryat's Crambe, or His Coleworte Twice Sodden*.

However, it was another book that was to change the British way of eating. The book is entitled *Coryat's Crudities:* [deep breath for the subtitle] *Hastily gobbled up in Five Months Travels in France, Savoy, Italy … and Switzerland, some parts of Germany and the Netherlands*.

Coryat's fascinating account of his tour of Europe in 1608 – he was perhaps the first man to go on the Grand Tour – has led him to be described as the English Marco Polo. In Venice, he notes,

'Almost all the wives, widows and maids do walk abroad with their breasts all naked, and many of them have their backs also naked almost even to the middle … a fashion methinks very unseemly …' Mind you, he found the heat so intolerable that he 'was forced to lie stark naked most commonly every night, and could not endure any clothes at all upon me.' He writes:

I observed a custom in all those Italian cities and towns through which I passed, that is not used in any other country that I saw in my travels, neither do I think that any other nation of Christendom doth use it, but only Italy. The Italian, and also most strangers that are commorant in Italy, do always, at their meals use a little fork when they cut the meat; for while with their knife, which they hold in one hand, they cut the meat out of the dish, they fasten their fork which they hold in their other hand, upon the same dish, so that whatsoever he be that sitteth in the company of any others at meat, should unadvisedly touch the dish of meat with his fingers, from which all at the table doe cut he will give occasion of offence unto the company as having transgressed the lawes of good manners, insomuch for his error he shall be at least browbeaten, if not reprehended in words.

This forme of feeding I understand is generally used in all places of Italy, their forks being for the most part made of iron or steel, and some of silver, but those are used only by gentlemen. The reason of this their curiosity, is because the Italian cannot by any means endure to have his dish touched with fingers, seeing all men's fingers are not alike clean.

Coryat became an ardent fork fan, using it upon his return to Britain. He must have been considered a bit of a freak at the table, and acquired the nickname 'Furciver', Latin for 'fork-bearer'.

Coryat certainly aroused curiosity among the British. Forks began to sell, though five years later, in 1617, Ben Jonson did his best to prevent the use of this particular utensil:

> Forks! What are they?
> The laudable use of forks,
> Brought into custom here, as they are in Italy,
> To the sparing of napkins.

Many believed that God had provided us at birth with forks – we know them as our fingers. By the 1660s sets of knives and forks were being made. Coryat died of dysentery in 1617 while travelling in Suryat. Sadly, he never quite saw his true impact upon the lifestyles of his countrymen. Incidentally, his description of how the Italians shielded themselves from the sun gave us the word umbrella. Great man.

7. THE FRIDGE AND FREEZER

....

Including all things dairy.

Freaky fridge facts

In 1948 just 2 per cent of households in Britain owned a refrigerator. Even in 1959 only 13 per cent of homes had one, compared with 96 per cent in America. But this next bit is even more alarming: in the 1700s when the word 'refrigeratory' was coined, no one had a fridge. It meant 'something that cools' – but no one really had anything that cooled.

In the 1820s brewers came up with a cabinet for keeping food cool; they called it the refrigerator. The electric-powered household device was available from the end of the First World War. Refrigerator became frigerator and then Fridgidaire started making fridges.

The word 'fridge' was considered a bit common; like 'loo' instead of lavatory. Cookbooks in the 1970s still shied away from the colloquial 'fridge', preferring 'refrigerator'.

What did we do before we had the fridge?

Florence Greenberg's Cookery Book (published in 1947) had the answers for readers who had yet to own a refrigerator. There were quite a few of them. Here Florence provides her readers with storage advice.

Meat. Cover with a wire gauze frame; then see that the frame fits the dish tightly, so that flies are unable to enter. Covers must be kept scrupulously clean

Milk in hot weather. Place bottles of milk in a basin of cold water; cover bottles with muslin, the ends of which should rest in water. Stand in a draught.

Cheese. Wrap the cheese in greaseproof paper, then in damp muslin and hang it in a cool, airy place. Or simply wrap the cheese in muslin wrung out in vinegar. For cooking leave the ends of cheese until really dry, then grate them, place in a screw-topped jar, and keep in a cool larder.

Vegetables. Keep vegetables in a vegetable rack. Wrap green vegetables in newspaper and put lettuce in a saucepan or bowl. Cover, and stand in a cool dry place or store in plastic bags. Remove the tops of the carrots, turnips, parsnips, and radishes before placing in the vegetable rack. Put onions and shallots in a string bag and hang them where the air can get at them.

No food should ever be put away on the dish on which it is served.

Inspect the larder daily and see that it is in good order.

> Florence Greenberg also offered
> 'advice regarding the length of time
> for keeping canned foods'.
> Canned milk, fruit, and fish in tomato sauce
> could last one year. Vegetables, honey
> and jam could last two years. Canned
> meat and fish in oil could last five years.

Ice cream comes to the streets

Ice cream was a gastronomic novelty of the 17th century, the food of kings and aristocrats. Such ice cream is not a taste most of us know, but the Foodie's historian friend Andrea Zuvich says, 'Let me tell you, it certainly is a world away from Ben & Jerry's! I sampled it when I was participating in a 17th century re-enactment at Bolsover Castle. I played one of the Cavendish women. The ice cream was bitty, stringy and lumpy. I have yet to make it myself, but it was sweet, and not at all as soft and creamy as we are able to have today. It was also heavily perfumed with the orange blossom.'

It was not until the early 1850s that ice cream became a successful product sold by street vendors (who included entrepreneurial dairy farmers). In the parks and markets of London, there were the cries, 'Raspberry cream! Iced raspberry cream, ha'penny a glass!'

These ice creams, or street ices as they were also known, were sold in very small glasses which the vendor dipped into a large vessel transported by horse and cart. There were no spoons – customers ate with their fingers. Many of them were trying ice cream for the first time, and remarked upon the feeling that 'it had snowed in their bellies'.

In 1851, one commentator wrote that street ices 'were somewhat of a failure last year … but this year they seem likely to succeed.' Meanwhile, Italian immigrants to Britain brought their own recipes for ice cream, as well as their passion for food. Cheerfully selling ice cream wrapped in paper from their carts they would cry *Occhi poco!* ('little eyes!' – as in, feast your little eyes on this delicious ice cream). To their audience who hadn't a clue what *occhi poco* meant, the Italian ice cream sellers became known as *hokey-pokey* men. Many claim to have invented the ice cream cone, but it is most likely to have been the Italians in Britain at the end of the 1850s.

A hundred years later there were 20,000 ice cream vans in Britain – a number that would decline once supermarkets mastered the ice cream trade.

How to stop an ice cream bore

When someone is being boring on the subject of making ice cream, swiftly stop him by saying, 'In China, a man with sexual desire is said to be *eating ice cream with the eyes*. Or, in simple Chinese, 他吃冰淇淋, 他的眼睛.' That should do the trick.

Famous last words

Lou Costello – the funny, chubby half of US comedy duo Abbott and Costello – suffered a heart attack on 26 February 1959 and was admitted to Doctors Hospital in Beverley Hills. On 13 March he was visited by his manager, Eddie Sherman. Lou persuaded Eddie to nip off to a nearby drugstore to get him a strawberry ice cream soda. After relishing it, Lou declared, 'That was the best ice cream soda I ever tasted.' Then he died of a heart attack.

The cows of St James's

Open the fridge door and inside you'll find a pint of milk. Such convenience didn't exist in the 19th century, of course.

If you lived in London's West End you might have taken a stroll to St James's Park. The Home Secretary granted permission for milkmen and women to bring their cows to the park. There were eight cow stands in the summer, but only half that number in the winter. The customers were mostly young women and young children brought by their nannies (and carrying their own china cups). Many men did not consider fresh milk to be good for the health, and thought it sickly.

Meanwhile, milk sellers in smocks would also go with cans of milk to places like Battersea Fields, Clapham Common, Camberwell Green and Hampstead Heath. They bought skimmed milk from the dairies and then watered it down even further before flogging it for half a penny a pint. Though it wasn't a pint – the measures were usually false.

The cow that was milked the most (by an ad agency)

It was New York and the World's Fair of 1939. Borden, the US dairy farmers, created an eye-catching and innovative exhibit for the event. Described as a 'Rotolactor', it was a massive, glass-enclosed turntable upon which cows were milked by automatic machines. The spectacle was futuristic and a hit with fairgoers, but it was only used twice a day – during milking. Crowds were thin in between.

Searching for a solution, Borden's ad agency scanned a list of questions asked by visitors. They were amazed to find that six out of every ten asked, 'Which cow is Elsie?' Elsie did not really exist – or rather, she was a cartoon character used in magazine ads for Borden milk. The agency needed an Elsie, so went to the Borden herd of 150 cows. They picked a good-natured, big-eyed Jersey who was called You'll Do Lobelia. She was renamed Elsie, put on the Rotolactor between milkings, and the greatest-ever bovine star was born. By the time the fair closed in 1940, Elsie was the star attraction.

She became the guest of honour at gala dinners and in 1940 starred in an RKO feature, *Little Men*. Her life was a series of cross-country appearances in her custom eighteen-wheeler (later dubbed the 'Cowdillac'). But on 16 April 1941, while on her way to the Theater District of New York City, her truck was hit from behind by another truck while at traffic lights.

Elsie/You'll do Lobelia suffered neck and spine injuries and was returned to her home at the Walker-Gordon Farm in Plainsboro, New Jersey. The vet determined that she could not be saved so she was put to sleep and buried on the farm. A headstone was erected at the farm's entrance, praising her as 'one of the great Elsies of our time'. Borden quietly christened a new Elsie.

The cowboy's cow of Hollywood

The Sunset Tower is an imposing Art Deco structure in Hollywood, and when the hotel was built in 1929–31 it became the city's first quake-proof building. It boasted electrical outlets in every bathroom and floor-to-ceiling windows with panoramic views.

Those who lived here included Clark Gable and Carole Lombard, Jean Harlow, and Truman Capote, who wrote, 'I am living in a very posh establishment, the Sunset Tower, which, or so the local gentry tell me, is where every scandal that ever happened, happened.'

Quite a madhouse in its day. Former residents included John Wayne, who kept a cow on the balcony of his apartment there. When he served visitors coffee, Wayne would wave towards the window, beyond which his beast paraded, and drawl, 'Help ya self ter milk.'

Bacon's final experiment

Those who have given their lives in the pursuit of good food include (the aptly named) Francis Bacon, the 17th-century scientist and philosopher. One winter's day he was travelling by horse-drawn carriage through the streets of London on his way to his home in Highgate and gazing out at the falling snow. 'Stop the carriage,' he shouted.

Bacon, it transpired, was in the midst of a Eureka moment: he wondered whether snow (or ice) might be as effective as salt when it came to preserving meat. With all the fervour and uncontrollable zeal that we have come to expect of mad scientists, he bought a hen from a woman and had her slaughter the bird and remove its guts. Perhaps a crowd gathered to observe Bacon as he now stuffed snow into the carcass of the hen.

It would be uplifting to conclude that Bacon went on to invent the first freezer. Alas, the ending is not so happy. During the course of his experiment Bacon caught a severe cold. He was so ill that he was taken to the nearby home of a friend who lived in Highgate and was placed into 'a damp bed that had not been layn-in about a yeare before'. In other words, he received the sort of treatment he'd dished out to the hen. His cold got worse and within a few days Bacon died.

8. THE STORE CUPBOARD

···

Bovril: the soldier's sustenance

The Franco-Prussian War of 1870–71 produced two significant incidents in food history.

One was the consumption of the contents of the zoo in Paris: the animals were eaten. At the time, the city was under siege by Wilhelm I's troops and food was scarce. In order to survive, the Parisians were forced to eat rats, cats and dogs. But this being Paris, the restaurants remained open; it was business as usual, though with limited supplies. And so the restaurateurs turned to the live inhabitants of the zoo. Suddenly, zebra, giraffe, elephant and gnu were on the menu, roasted, sautéed, poached and grilled.

The second foodie outcome of the war was the creation of Bovril, the meat extract which is similar to Marmite. At the beginning of the war, Napoleon III decreed that a million cans of beef were needed to feed his troops. Rustling up such an order is no mean feat, as you can imagine. John Lawson Johnston, a Scotsman who lived in Canada, found the solution.

Large quantities of beef were available across the British Dominions and South America, but its transport and storage were problematic. Therefore Johnston created 'Johnston's Fluid Beef', to meet the needs of the French people and Napoleon. Mixed with boiling water, Johnston's Fluid Beef became beef tea.

It wasn't the most appetising of names and the product was renamed Bovril: *bov* being Latin for cow or ox; the *vril* suffix coming from Edward George Bulwer-Lytton's then-popular 'lost race' novel *The Coming Race*. The plot revolves around a superior race of people, the 'Vril-ya', whose powers come from an electromagnetic substance named 'Vril'.

By 1888, over 3,000 British public houses, grocers and chemists were selling Bovril. It fed soldiers during the world wars.

Beef tea is sold in football stadiums all over Britain, and in the early 20th century an advertising campaign depicted Pope Leo XIII seated on his throne, bearing a mug of Bovril, with the slogan: 'The Two Infallible Powers – The Pope & Bovril'.

On matters concerning the salt pot and pepper mill

Why are salt and pepper the only spices we put on the dinner table?
Tradition mainly. Other countries might have crushed chillies or dried herbs. In the UK some companies are now selling 'spice mixes' to shake on at the table.

Why do salt and sweet flavours work so well together, e.g. salted caramel and salted chocolate?
There is no ready explanation for this. It may be that you are getting different 'sensory hits' during eating, which might increase consumer interest.

Why does salt bring out the flavour of food?
This happens for two reasons:

1. Salt can literally 'salt out' flavours. This means that it effectively pushes out of the product more of the volatile flavour.
2. The aroma (smell of food) can be enhanced by tastes that are 'consonant' with the flavour – these are tastes that you expect.

So a salty taste makes you think that volatile savoury flavours are stronger.

To demonstrate these points, why not try the below recipe for chocolate cremosa? The cremosa – a rich chocolate mousse – is sprinkled with salt and then given a splash of good quality olive oil. Yes, olive oil. You think it cannot – will not – work, yet it is divine. It is a sensory revelation and will bring you immense pleasure.

The recipe is courtesy of Adam Byatt, chef-patron of Trinity in Clapham, south-west London.

It was possibly the Spanish who first paired chocolate with olive oil. However, it is also said that when Italian (and French) confectioners were making chocolate a sweet rather than a savoury spice, they combined it with the oil, probably in an experiment to improve taste and also because butter was expensive at the time, and not prevalent in warmer parts of Europe. The oil also produces an appetising gloss.

Chocolate cremosa with olive oil and salt

Ingredients:
For the crème anglaise:
250ml (9fl oz) whole milk
125ml (4½fl oz) double cream
1 vanilla pod, scraped and seeds removed
115g (4oz) sugar
10 egg yolks

For the cremosa:
Crème anglaise
150g (5½oz) good quality 70 per cent cocoa solids chocolate
(Adam suggests Valrhona)

Garnish:

Maldon salt

Good quality extra virgin olive oil

Method:

1. Boil the milk, cream and vanilla seeds. Pour this hot mixture over the egg yolks and sugar while whisking to stop scrambled egg forming.
2. Return the custard mixture to a pan and cook over a low heat until thickened like custard.
3. Using a blender, blend the chocolate and crème anglaise together until glossy.
4. Place in a plastic container, allow to cool and refrigerate overnight.
5. Serve a large tablespoon of the chocolate cremosa, sprinkle with salt and coat the cremosa with a high quality olive oil, to your taste.

Note: As an option, toast fennel seeds in a dry pan, cool slightly, add the salt; sprinkle over the cremosa.

> When making soup, season with salt – a little at the beginning and more at the end. However, if you over-salt, add a slice or two of raw potato. Potato absorbs salt – a good mash, for instance, needs a decent seasoning of salt. Most starchy carbs, like rice or pasta, would have the same effect. Or add a teaspoon of brown sugar. Why would this work? It's due to taste suppression; sweetness suppresses your perception of salty taste.

Ketchup

Ketchup, catchup or catsup, derives from *ke-chiap* (sometimes written *ke-tsiap*), which was a pickled fish sauce popular in China. European traders loved the sauce and brought it west with them in the 17th century. Or does the name come from Indonesia, where *kicap* (or *kecap* or *ketjap*) was a sauce made of brined shellfish, herbs and spices?

Whatever the exact origin of the term, it was mostly catsup in Britain. Jonathan Swift's poem Panegyric On The Dean (1730) refers to it:

> She sent her priests in wooden shoes
> From haughty Gaul to make ragouts;
> Instead of wholesome bread and cheese,
> To dress their soups and fricassees;
> And, for our home-bred British cheer,
> Botargo, catsup, and caviare.

Was Swift referring to tomato catsup? No, probably mushroom. In the 1800s if you nipped down to Butler's Herb and Seed Shop, in Henrietta Street, Covent Garden, upon the shelves you could find 'excellent mushroom catsup'. Cooks of the day wrote recipes for catsups of tomato, oyster, cockle and mussel, and cucumber.

In the early 1800s, the tomato-based version of the sauce quickly became popular in the United States. At first, it was made primarily by local farmers. By 1837, though, at least one company was making ketchup and distributing it around the nation.

The H.J. Heinz Company didn't start producing the sauce

until 1876. The company originally called it catsup, but soon switched to ketchup to stand out, and now we all call it ketchup.

The influence of American cookery writers would eventually see the demise of mushroom ketchup and the rise of tomato ketchup, partly because of its flavour and also because of its versatility – as the cookbook authors pointed out, it could be used in stews, fricassees and other dishes.

Until the 1900s catsup recipes were frequent in cookbooks. Once commercial catsup was available, the recipes vanished – why go to the fuss of making it at home when it was available to buy (and inexpensive)?

An early catsup recipe

In his *Universal Recipe Book*, published in 1814, Richard Alsop gives a recipe for Catsup:

'Take two gallons of stale strong beer or ale, the stronger and staler the better', which is then mixed with 1lb anchovies, ½oz each of cloves and mace, ¼oz of pepper, six large roots of ginger, 1lb shallots, and 'two quarts or more of flap mushrooms, well rubbed and picked'. These ingredients are boiled for an hour, strained and bottled. 'One spoonful of this catsup to a pint of melted butter gives an admirable taste and colour and is by many preferred to the best Indian soy.'

Alsop commended it as an 'excellent Catsup that will keep good for more than twenty years'. Sell-by dates would not be introduced until the 1970s (by Marks and Spencer).

While we're thinking about ketchup, this might be a good time to consider ...

The hot dog
by 'Hot' Doug Sohn

It is said that the greatest hot dogs in the world can be found in Chicago, Illinois, at a restaurant called Hot Doug's. It's a restaurant with a sub-title, too: 'Sausage Superstore and Encased Meat Emporium'. Chef-proprietor is Doug Sohn. While hot dogs are perceived as junk food, Doug delivers gastronomy. Queues of gourmets line up outside his restaurant, waiting to be fed by this man.

In 2006, Hot Doug's got into heaps of trouble for serving foie gras-based sausages and condiments following the banning of foie gras by the city of Chicago. Sohn flouted the law by developing a 'celebrity' dog made with foie gras, naming it after Alderman Joe Moore – the man calling for the ban – and selling the 'Joe Moore' dog during the ban. Doug was eventually fined $250 and 30lbs (14kg) of foie gras were confiscated from the restaurant. The ban was repealed in May 2008 and the foie gras items were brought back into the restaurant's rotating menu line-up.

Anyhow, the hot dog doesn't get enough credit. I've never seen it mentioned in a cookbook, and that's unfair because it is loved by zillions. So I asked Doug, the master of the dog, to tell me about the hot dog so that its name (and his) could appear in print. Here's Doug ...

I love food, all kinds of food. Whether it's foie gras, a delicate piece of fish, a warm stew or a bag of potato chips, it doesn't matter – good food makes me happy. But if I had to choose the one food that makes me the happiest, it's a hot dog. Hot dog, frankfurter, tube steak, wiener ... call it what you want. To me it's the perfect food. It's easy to eat, it's inexpensive, it can be served in a variety of ways and, most importantly, it tastes good. Really, really good. It's meat, fat and salt rolled up into one tidy package.

Growing up in Chicago, hot dogs become a staple of one's diet, in particular the all-beef Chicago-style hot dog with all the toppings. A classic Chicago dog is a natural-casing all-beef frankfurter, either steamed or char-grilled, and served in a steamed poppy seed bun. It's topped with yellow mustard, onions (either fresh or grilled), tomatoes, dill pickle spear, neon-green sweet relish (a Chicago-only product as far as I know) and a dash of celery salt. Spicy pickled sport peppers are optional – I usually skip those as I think the spice overtakes too many of the other flavours. That's one of the great things about the Chicago dog: there are enough condiments that you can truly customise it to your liking.

The Chicago-style hot dog came about as not only an inexpensive lunch for the non-wealthy (i.e., virtually everybody), but also as an amalgam of the European immigrants who settled in Chicago. The main influences are German, Polish, Eastern European and Italian. The condiments reflect these people and the cultures in which they grew up. And, with Chicago being the primary cattle stockyard for the entire country, it's natural that the hot dog was made from beef.

Unlike most cities I've visited, hot dogs are a meal in Chicago. It's not just a snack that you have on your way to a proper meal. They are ubiquitous. Allegedly, the Chicago area boasts more hot dog restaurants than McDonald's, Wendy's and Burger King restaurants combined. It's part of the culture, it's part of your day-to-day life (and if it isn't, it certainly should be). They're also delicious. I do love having a hot dog no matter what city I'm in. And the one thing that most foreign hot dogs usually have in common is that the bread/bun is delicious, the mustard and/or toppings are top notch and the actual hot dog is terrible. I wouldn't say inedible, but awfully close. This has been especially true in Paris. And yet, I almost always have one when I'm there. I just can't help it.

> Place marshmallows in a bag with bread
> to stop both going stale and hard.

What on earth do astronauts eat?

The store cupboard is all that an astronaut has when it comes to food. You and I can pop down to the butcher or fishmonger, using it as an excuse to nip into the pub for a quick sharpener. We can whiz into the supermarket for this or that. Our milk might be delivered fresh by the milkman. More fresh produce might come courtesy of Derek, the driver of Ocado's onion-coloured van.

NASA's astronauts don't have these luxuries. They can take fresh food on a mission, but it needs to be eaten quite soon after launch. Most space food is in a rehydratable form: it has had its water removed, and hot water must be added to it just before it is eaten. Cereals (including Rice Krispies and Corn Flakes) are packaged with non-fat dry milk and sugar; water is then added to the mix. Likewise beef goulash, scrambled eggs, macaroni cheese and prawn cocktail (cold water for the last one). Fruit and fish comes in cans. Other foods, such as casseroles, and condiments like ketchup, mayonnaise, Tabasco and the American's much-loved taco sauce, are in pouches.

Drinks, which include coffee, tea and cider, are in powdered form – just add water. Liquid pepper (suspended in olive oil) and liquid salt (dissolved in water) come in polyethylene dropper bottles.

Astronauts have fewer red blood cells while in space and iron from food goes into those cells. If they had foods high in iron, they would have health problems, so foods with minimal iron amounts are chosen. Sodium and vitamin D affect bone. Too much salt can lead to bone loss. There's no natural sunlight so no vitamin D. Therefore, they require vitamin D supplements while on their trips.

If you are an astronaut, cooking a meal is a 15-step process with NASA guidelines. The first six go like this:

1. Collect meal tray and utensils.
2. Display preselected meal on the computer.
3. Locate food using location display function.
4. Prepare food items for heating.
5. Place items to be heated in oven.
6. Enter cook control codes and press 'start'.

What is the food of love?

'Food of love for me is not anything glamorous or sexy like caviar or oysters or even slow-poached Scottish lobster but something much more simple. Dave my stepdad was amazing with me but his culinary repertoire was severely limited to two dishes: sardines on toast and beans on toast.

'We'd sit at the dinner table together and have hot beans on toast with loads of fresh butter and HP sauce. It is still my comfort food today and takes me back to being a small boy, and really understanding how food can play a massive part in love and fond memories.'

—Jason Atherton, chef-proprietor,
Pollen Street Social, London

THE FOODIE

9. THE SPICE RACK

The science of heat on the palate

Why do cold things like mustard and peppers taste 'hot'?

This is due to 'chemesthesis' and our trigeminal senses, the nerves for which are wrapped around the papillae on our tongues, but also have branches to the eyes and nose. Trigeminal senses include heat from mustard and chilli as well as cooling sensations from mint and the pungency of onions. These senses can also induce 'cheese sweats' around the eyes.

Why do we react to spicy heat – e.g. chillies, curries – and what causes the reaction? Is it a type of allergy? Why can some people tolerate very spicy foods while others can't?

This is due to chemesthesis but the level of sensitivity varies among different individuals. Some people are 'supertasters' who have more papillae on their tongues, which are surrounded by more trigeminal nerves. Therefore they perceive chemical irritants more easily, and spicy foods constitute a chemical irritant.

Three recipes for Mauritian chutney

In the summer of 2012 I got a call from Barnaby Jones, then the executive chef of Le Touessrok, a five-star hotel in Mauritius, set beside the Indian Ocean, with about ten restaurants.

Barnaby said, 'Do you want to come here, bring the family, stay for a couple of weeks and write a book about our food?'

I said, 'I can't think of anything worse!' We took the next flight.

Here are three easy-peasy recipes for chutney that feature in *Le Touessrok Cookbook*.

Coconut chutney

Ingredients: 1 firm dry coconut removed from shell, 1 tbsp fresh mint, 1 green chilli, 2 tbsp water, 2 tsp lemon juice.

Method:

Place the coconut, mint, chopped chilli and a couple of tablespoons of water in a food processor (or use a stick blender) and blend until a rough paste is formed.

Season with the lemon juice, and salt and pepper to your taste.

Tomato and coriander chutney

Ingredients: 3 large tomatoes, 1 small red onion, 1 bunch fresh coriander, 1 garlic clove, 1 small red chilli, olive oil.

Method:

Place all the ingredients in a food processor (or use a stick blender) and blend to a rough purée. Season with salt and pepper to your taste.

Potato chutney

Ingredients: 3 large potatoes, 2 chopped dried red chillies, 2 tbsp olive oil, 2 spring onions, 1 tbsp chopped parsley, juice of 1 lemon.

Method

Peel the potatoes and boil slowly until cooked through. Remove from the water and drain until dry.

Crush the potatoes and mix thoroughly with the chopped red chillies, spring onions, parsley, olive oil and lemon juice. Season with salt and pepper to your taste.

Dealing with spice bores

When a pedant is boring you on his knowledge of all things spice, end his monologue by asking him, 'Do you like gamboge?' He will look at you blankly. In the curries of Sri Lanka (formerly Ceylon) gamboge is used as a souring and thickening agent in white curries, fish and meat preparations, and certain vegetable curries. It can be replaced by a capful or two of vinegar.

The mysterious curry cookbook

The Madras Cookery Book was first published in India by Higginbothams way back in 1882, and is the height and width of a one-pound bag of sugar, though nowhere close in terms of weight. A more quaint and dainty cookbook you will never come across.

It has intrigue and mystery: its author, as described on the front cover, is 'An Old Lady-Resident'. Who was the food-fascinated, elderly woman who compiled this feast of colonial dishes? To this day her identity remains unknown.

Perhaps the author was a relative of Abel Higginbotham, a librarian who left Britain and went to India, it is said, as a stowaway, later to open a bookshop (India's first) and then a successful publishing house.

'Wooden ladles are best for stirring rice,' the old lady tells her readers, 'a large porcelain cullender [sic], a coarse hair sieve and a lemon squeezer, should always be at hand where Indian cookery is done ... The young house-keeper or cook, or whoever is engaged in the all-important task of getting ready the meal, will do well to first place upon the table all the ingredients mentioned in the recipe, then their method of preparations will be easily and quickly managed.'

There are scores of recipes, including one for stewed sheep's tongues and another for a one-pot dish called 'buffado', which begins, 'Kill a good, fat duck and clean it well …' Please read on for two recipes – 'ding-dong' and 'pudding à l'elegante' – written as they appear in *The Madras Cookery Book*. You can make them at home and be transported back to the glory days of the Raj.

Ding-dong

Required – 1lb of good tender fat beef, 10 dried chillies ground, 1 stick of saffron, one pod garlic, 2 tablespoonfuls of soft sugar, 1 tablespoonful of salt, bread and butter.

Method – Cut the beef in thin slices, grind all the currystuff ingredients to a smooth paste and mix with the salt and keep by; rub the sugar into the beef first and then the ground currystuff; put away for six hours and fry as it is wanted, serve hot. A nice relish to curry or bread and butter.

THE FOODIE'S NOTE: think of this as a lovely canapé. Use rump steak (remember to finely slice it) and brown sugar. Marinate in the fridge overnight. Once cooked, each slice can be rolled and held in place with a cocktail stick.

Pudding à l'elegante

Required – Slices of light white bread, some orange marmalade, 1 pint of warm milk, 4 eggs, wine sauce.

Method – Cut thin slices from a light white bread and line a pudding mould with them, putting in alternate layers of the bread and orange marmalade or any other preserve, till the mould is nearly full. Pour over all the milk in which the eggs well-beaten have been mixed. Cover the mould with a cloth, and boil for an hour and a half. Serve with wine sauce.

THE FOODIE'S NOTE: This is easy-to-make, sweet comfort food. Of course, cream was not part of the diet in the intense heat of India. But this pudding is enriched by using a mix of half-cream, half-milk. In a saucepan, and over a gentle heat, bring the cream-milk mix to the boil before blending it in a large bowl with the beaten eggs.

You could also cook this pudding in a Pyrex dish or casserole dish; cover it with baking paper, and bake for about an hour in an oven preheated to 120°C. Serve with custard, cream or vanilla ice cream.

What is the food of love?

'When I was growing up in Calabria, I remember summertime with my grandmother. Nonna Francesca would dry the chilli under the sun and then make a powder and, in turn, this powder would be used to make salami. I remember the smell when she crushed the chilli under a mortar. It was strong; so strong it would make Nonna cry and I'd cry with her. One summer she got a Moulinex and crushed lots of chilli, and when she removed the machine's cap we all cried! Chilli is not just the food of love. It's an aphrodisiac and contains capsaicin, which is good for the heart.'

—Francesco Mazzei, L'Anima, London

10. THE TOASTER

The Grand Dame

Although Auguste Escoffier was a married man, there is no question that the chef was besotted with Nellie Melba, the Australian opera singer. After all, he named Pêche Melba after Nellie, though the forerunner to this ice dish was inspired by a clergyman and named 'Pêche Cardinale', with a raspberry coulis around the peach to represent the red of the cardinal's robe. Nellie's dish had vanilla ice cream with the peach.

But to toast ... Nellie visited London in 1897 and during her trip she was taken ill, suffering a cold. Cesar Ritz, the creator of London hotels The Ritz and The Savoy, had invited her to recuperate at his home in the London suburb of Hampstead. Nellie had accepted. She was in the garden, doubtless wrapped in shawls, when Escoffier arrived, perhaps in flirtatious mood. Poor Nellie was hungry but her sore throat prevented her from eating anything other than soup.

Escoffier dashed to the kitchen and within a few minutes returned with a plate of what would become known as Melba toast. He had toasted the bread, sliced it through the middle lengthways, and voila: the toast was so thin it could do no damage to the singer's cherished throat. 'We shall call it Melba toast,' announced Cesar. This could have done little to impress Cesar's wife. Some months earlier Escoffier had done the same trick with the toast and the two men had named it 'Marie toast', after Mrs Ritz.

In the mid-1920s the American actress Ethel Barrymore was prescribed a diet of Melba toast, and overnight the Melba toast industry was born.

Can toast be drunk?

It can. In Victorian times the British working classes drank 'toast water', using it during illness as a form of nourishment. The recipe goes like this: 'Toast a piece of bread thoroughly browned to its centre without being burnt, put it into a jug, pour boiling water upon it, cover over and allow it to stand and steep until it has cooled; it will then be fit to drink.'

Toast water benefits from a dollop of blackcurrant jam, added to the jug before the boiling water.

Toast Day

Yes, Britain has a National Toast Day. The first one took place in February 2014. Britons are asked on this day to tweet about how they take their toast. Golden? Brown? Burnt to a cinder? Toast is considered to be our favourite feel-good food and Britain's most loved food smell because it triggers memories of happiness.

What is the food of love?

'My "food of love" is Shepherd's Pie, a simple yet deeply delicious dish and the ideal crowd food. There is something quietly perfect and warmly nostalgic about a forkful of luxurious, succulent meat nestled beneath a mound of fluffy potato with a crisp topping. It needs no accompaniment other than friends and a great bottle of Burgundy!

'I prepared the following version for a gathering of friends and family on New Year's Eve with simple ingredients found on my doorstep in the mountains of Switzerland.

'I cut, rather than chopped, into tiny pieces the leftovers from a best end of Simmental veal, a mountain breed, mother-reared and cooked on the bone two days beforehand. Into the basin I mixed in some barely cooked, sweetly incandescent mushrooms and laid the mixture between two layers of glossy mashed potatoes, creamed lightly with Gruyère milk and a couple of knobs of butter. It was finished with a sprinkling of grated cheese, Tomme from the Valais. This is a delicately flavoured, hard cheese produced locally from milk collected in April and May from the Simmental cows which graze on the mountainside here.

'This pie proved a wonderful antidote to the excesses of Christmas and proved that simple, humble comfort food, lovingly prepared, is hard to beat.'

—Michel Roux, OBE

11. THE FRUIT BOWL

....

'The banana plant is large and fine, it rises about ten
or twelve foot out of the ground, and has very large
leaves of an oval figure. It bears a fruit as long as
one's hand, and of the bigness of the fist of a child
of four years old. It is outwardly yellow when it is
ripe, and white within, a little clammy like the inside
of apricot and of a delicate and excellent flavour.'

—François Leguat,
A New Voyage to the East Indies (1708)

The Banana by Marcus Wareing

*By way of introduction, Marcus Wareing is chef-patron of his epony-
mously named restaurant at the Berkeley Hotel in Knightsbridge.
One day I sat entranced as he talked to me about the banana. Over
to Marcus ...*

When I was growing up, Dad had a fruit and veg business, so you
might think that means I was raised on the finest quality produce.
Not a bit of it. Dad supplied to school kitchens in the North West,
and those pupils ate well because they got the best stuff.

But what Dad brought home was the fruit and veg he couldn't
sell. There was always something wrong with it – it would be old
or over-ripe or falling apart. The bananas were no exception: often
manky and covered in black spots.

A popular dessert in our house was sliced bananas with a

piping hot, home-made custard, and if it was a warm summer's day, we'd have the same thing but with the custard cold.

Years later, I realised that the best bananas you can buy are the ones that Dad couldn't sell, where the skin is covered with small, black spots and speckles. Quite simply, the banana that might seem over-ripe to many people is, in fact, the most flavoursome. When the fruit is getting older, its taste intensifies and improves with maturity. So you can judge a banana by its skin.

Unfortunately, supermarkets and many shoppers have got it all wrong. They think that a good banana is one with a bright yellow skin and very firm fruit. Utter rubbish. It might look 'beautiful', but I'm sorry, the fruit will have no flavour whatsoever.

If you are in the supermarket and want bananas, head straight for the reduced section, and then rummage around for old bananas at a knock-down price and put them in your trolley. I tend to buy from Waitrose, but I'm not fussed about the bananas' country of origin – a banana is a banana, no matter where it comes from.

If you are one of those people who likes to buy green bananas, then fine, but only if you know how to store them correctly. People often keep them in the fridge, which is wrong. My Dad would always wrap bananas in newspaper and then stash them in a dark place that was not too warm and not too cold. Lack of light and ambient temperature are essential factors in storage.

Then you come across people who chuck away bananas just as they are reaching their most magnificent taste. It is absolute stupidity (and a waste of money) to bin a banana when it starts to go brown. Simply peel it, put the fruit into a freezer bag and keep it in the freezer for a smoothie at a later date.

Then there are the varying degrees of ripeness, and remember the banana is unusual in that it is a fruit that is picked green and continues to ripen as it makes it way across the world towards Britain.

If you want a peeling banana (to eat 'raw') or to slice it, the skin should be just yellow. For a smoothie, the skin needs to have those black spots which tell you that the fruit will have a bit of texture to it.

We talk about *cooking* bananas, but that's probably the wrong word to use. This fruit is not like an apple, which you might put on to the heat to transform it from a hard texture to soft. With the banana, it is already soft enough to eat so what we are actually doing is warming it through.

A delicious dish is pan-fried banana, where the fruit should have some body to it but not be absolutely knackered. In the frying pan heat a large knob of butter and some demerara sugar until it turns into a caramel; throw in your bananas and, as soon as they start to colour, chuck in some dark rum. Rum and banana are the perfect combination – it's a spirit that amplifies the banana flavour. Let the alcohol burn off, remove from the pan, and serve with toasted flaked almonds on top and with ice cream. The trick about sautéing bananas is not to keep them in the pan for too long: they have a high water content and if too much water comes out, they'll turn to mush. I've never made banoffee pie (layers of biscuit, toffee, banana and cream) but if I were to, I think I'd purée the bananas rather than incorporate them in slices.

But my favourite of all is banana bread, which I used to make when I worked in America. There, we'd serve it for breakfast. Here in Britain, we serve it at tea. Again, the key to success of this cake is the ripeness of the banana – they need to be over-ripe!

Marcus Wareing's Banana Bread

Ingredients:

2 large eggs, 1 tsp vanilla extract, 1 tsp almond extract, 300g (10oz) strong white bread flour, 1 tsp baking powder, ¼ tsp fine salt, 115g (4oz) softened unsalted butter, 100g (3½oz) caster sugar,

4 over-ripe bananas (with a total raw weight of about 550g/1¼lbs) peeled and mashed, 75g (2½oz) chopped walnuts.

Method:

Pre-heat the oven to 180°C (350°F/Gas 4).

In a bowl, whisk the eggs with the vanilla and almond extracts.

Sift the flour into a bowl and mix with the baking powder and salt.

Cream the butter and sugar together until light and fluffy. Pour in the egg–extract mixture and, very slowly, beat until completely incorporated.

Fold the mashed bananas into the mixture. Fold in the sifted dry ingredients and the walnuts (one-third at a time).

Pour the sloppy mixture into a greased loaf tin and cook for 55 minutes.

When it comes out of oven, check it is cooked through by inserting a skewer, which, when removed, should be clean.

Leave it to sit in the tin for 15 minutes before removing. Serve cold.

Which month, which orange?

The **tangerine** is in season from October to March; the **satsuma** from October to February; the **clementine** from November to February; **blood oranges** are in season in February and March; **Seville oranges** are ready to eat in January and February.

> To test the ripeness of a melon, gently press the root underneath with both thumbs. The aroma will generally give an accurate measure of the melon's ripeness. If it is over-ripe the melon will explode all over you.

On the subject of apple sauce

The apple is a magnificent thing, ranging in taste from sweet to sour, and is possibly Britain's favourite fruit. In the wrong hands it can become ghastly and is often spoiled when cooked. The trick is to keep your apples simple.

Ensure that you have an apple with a good deal of flavour. If you are shopping for apples in a supermarket, smell the fruit before you put it in your trolley. If an apple (or any other fruit or veg, for that matter) has no smell then it certainly won't have any flavour. That's a given. Discard the British notion that apples must be divided into 'cookers' and 'eaters': that sour apples should be cooked and sweet apples eaten raw. If you cook with sour apples then lots of sugar needs to be added to reduce the acidity. Cook with an apple that is delicious in its raw form. Cox's have a wonderful flavour but they also have a low water content so that when they cook they don't turn to mush.

Apple sauce is the perfect accompaniment to roast pork, and is also lovely with roasted goose and pheasant. It has to be one of the easiest accompaniments in the world to make but frequently it is overcooked, thereby losing flavour and changing the texture. In fact the secret of the sauce is to cook it rapidly.

Top and tail your apples, peel them, split them in half, core them, and then slice them wafer thin. Remember, the smaller the pieces, the faster they'll cook.

In a saucepan pour a little water – half a cup or so, just enough to stop the fruit scorching. Add a knob of butter and a squeeze of lemon juice and put the heat on high.

Place the sliced apples in the pan and cook rapidly. As they start to cook they'll release their own water. Cook for about 3 minutes.

Liquidise the mixture, and there you have it: not soggy, not lumpy, but very fresh and extremely tasty.

> To prevent chopped fruit from turning brown,
> squeeze lemon juice (or ascorbic acid) over it.
> Don't get the juice in your eyes – it really stings.

While sauce is on my mind...

A sauce boat, gravy boat or saucière is a boat-shaped pitcher in which sauce or gravy is served. It often sits on a matching plate, sometimes attached to the pitcher, to catch dripping sauce. Often sauce boats are really annoying. They never clean well in a dishwasher as the water can't get round the lips.

Sauce is a section within the traditional ranks of a professional kitchen, as in 'I'm on Sauce', usually meaning that the chef is cooking meat dishes and hot sauces. It's very different to 'I'm on *the* sauce.' If a chef is on the sauce you don't want him cooking your food.

Sauce boats became all the rage in the French Court of the 1690s. Silver sauce boats with two handles and two spouts were reported as early as 1690 and appear to have developed in response to the new and original *nouvelle cuisine*. French fashion was highly influential in 18th-century England, where such sauce boats were copied in English silver, and, from the 1740s, in English porcelain.

These boats do not float.

> Rather than removing the stones from cherries before making
> jam, simply cook them whole and pass the cooked purée through a
> potato ricer to remove the stones. This trick also works for prunes.

How to stop a fruit bore

If someone is being boring about fruit, stop him swiftly by saying. 'According to Macedonia folklore, the first fruit of the tree must not be eaten by a barren woman, but by one who has many children. Peasants of Austria and Bavaria believed that if you give the first fruit of a tree to a woman with child to eat, the tree will bring forth abundantly next year.'

If that doesn't work, point out that, while we all know that tomatoes are a fruit, some other 'vegetables' that are really fruits include peppers, chillies, cucumbers, aubergines and most squashes. They are fruits because you have to break the skin to get to the seeds or pips.

> Okra also goes by the name of lady's fingers and gombo. It is a tissue-healer and an hibiscus fruit.

Five 'different' fruits to grow at home according to botanist James Wong

Cocktail Kiwi (*Actinidia arguta*): Plant in spring, harvest in September. These rampant but hardy vines, which hail from North-East Asia and Siberia, will survive −35°C ... so they're ideal for the British climate! Mature plants produce up to 400 mini kiwis that are the size of grapes; the skins are edible and the flesh is sweet.

Chilean Guava (*Ugni molinae*): Plant in spring, harvest late summer. Said to have been Queen Victoria's favourite fruit, they are also known (or have been rebranded by Australian growers) as Tazziberries. A tiny punnet costs about a tenner.

Cape Gooseberry (*Physalis peruviana*): Seed March or April, harvest October to December. Despite their unusual appearance – each berry wrapped in a paper lantern – cape gooseberries are drought- and disease-resistant and need no pruning, training or fertilising.

Cucamelon (*Zehneria scabra syn. Melothria scabra*): Sow April, harvest August. These look like tiny watermelons, and taste of cucumber with a tinge of lime. They are perfect for patio pots or hanging baskets.

Pineapple guava (*Acca sellowiana*): Plant in spring, harvest late summer–autumn. These evergreen plants produce pink pompon flowers that have fleshy, edible, sweet-tasting petals. Plant in full sun, between two feijoas – this will ensure cross-pollination, which equals lots of fruit.

> Blending fresh passion fruit pulp in a food processor will allow you to separate the pips from the passion juice by passing the puréed mix through a sieve.

Why do the best raspberries come from Scotland?

Scotland can be cold, cloudy and windswept but it produces the finest raspberries Britain has to offer. In fact, it is precisely because of the weather that the raspberries are superior. Raspberries ripen too quickly in extreme heat. They need time for their flavour to become superb. In raspberry-growing areas like Blairgowrie, temperatures rarely go above 22°C, which is perfect for the raspberry.

> **Ten fruits that ripen after picking:**
> Apples, apricots, avocados, bananas,
> mangos, muskmelons, papayas,
> peaches, pears, persimmons.

Strawberries and cream

Tennis fans at Wimbledon munch their way through 110,000 punnets of strawberries, topped by 7,000 litres of cream. But what is the story of this fruit and dairy combination?

Let's go back to the 16th century, when Thomas (later to become Cardinal) Wolsey lived in Hampton Court Palace on the banks of the River Thames. Wolsey had yet to lose his home to King Henry VIII, and he entertained on a grand and extravagant scale. Life below stairs was not so cheerful. According to a Spanish visitor at the time – when the word 'veritable' was common – the palace kitchens were 'veritable hells, such is the stir and bustle in them … there is plenty of beer here, and they drink more than would fill the Valladolid river.'

From this veritable hell, gastronomic heaven was born. It was here that the strawberry is said to have first been paired with cream. Cardinal Wolsey himself takes the credit for the dish's creation, though I'm not so sure about that. Perhaps it was his chef's homage to both the red and white of the Tudor flag as well as ecclesiastical colours: the red a symbol of Jesus Christ's blood, the white representing purity and joy.

What is the food of love?

'When you are in love you don't really care about food.
But I can see myself sitting beneath a peach tree with the
woman I love, catching a ripe peach as it falls, and then
sharing it, of course. One big bite into the peach, and
the juices run everywhere. That is the food of love.'

—Pierre Koffmann, Koffmann's,
The Berkeley Hotel, London

12. THE LOCKED LARDER

....

Foods that we no longer eat, or are not supposed to eat because we might get arrested.

Turtle

To the modern gourmet, and most Britons, the thought of eating turtle is repugnant. After all, the reptile is an endangered species and it seems unfair that it can live happily in the seas for a hundred years or so and then be swiftly slaughtered for the plate.

Our ancestors, however, considered it one of the finest meats and it was the main ingredient for the most regal of soups. Mock turtle soup, incidentally, contains no turtle but is made from calf's head and for many years was a big seller (and the favourite soup of artist Andy Warhol, creator of the Campbell's Soup homage).

Colonisation saw the introduction of the turtle as a British food. It was shipped, while still alive, from places like the West Indies. Around 1760 Samuel Birch, whose successful catering company was responsible for catering at Lord Mayors' banquets, is said to have been the first to serve turtle soup in London, offering alongside it cayenne pepper, lemons and toast. Birch, who was known as Mr Pittypan, clearly won hearts through his food: he became Lord Mayor of London for a year from 1814. Where were the reptiles stored? Archaeologists have found the remains of turtles in a well in the City of London.

It was worth a pilgrimage to the City to taste turtle soup and 'fixings' (i.e. all the trimmings) at the Ship and Turtle, Leadenhall Street, established by 1377, rebuilt in 1887 and again in 1969. In its later years the pub was called Vino Veritas, but it closed and was demolished in 2008. For 465 years, from 1377 to 1835 it was run by a succession of widows. Turtle was on the menu during the 18th, 19th and early 20th centuries. During the Victorian era, the Ship and Turtle Tavern even supplied several of the West End club-houses. To assure the pub's patrons they were eating real turtle, turtles were kept on display in aquariums for everybody to see.

Elizabeth Raffald, a housekeeper and therefore well equipped to be the author of *The Experienced English Housekeeper*, tells her readers of the 1780s how to 'dress a turtle of a hundredweight'. That's 50kg, or 112lb, which is the weight of a small lamb.

Her gravy alone involved using two legs of veal and two shanks of beef. Different cuts of the turtle were cooked in various ways – stewed, fried, braised – with ingredients such as anchovies, mushroom 'catchup', truffles and Madeira.

Raffald's recipe is lengthy and time-consuming. Almost every part of the turtle makes it to the plate, including the head, which is braised and placed in the centre of the dish. She boasts that her turtle dish has 'often given great satisfaction'. She has an NB: 'Observe to kill your turtle the night before you want it, or very early next morning, that you may have all your dishes going on at a time.'

Ortolan: the thumb-sized bird beneath the napkin

For centuries, ortolan has been considered the haute-est of French haute cuisine, and while hunting of the bird has been banned in France since 1999, it is not illegal to eat it. It is most common in south-west France, and it has been reported that up to 50,000 orto-lans are thought to be killed each year by 1,500 poachers. Those arrested are liable for a £4,000 fine but usually they're given only a verbal warning.

What's so special about this bird that is the size of a thumb?

There is an almost religious ceremony surrounding the cooking and consumption of ortolan. The birds – which weigh less than an ounce – are fattened up on millet while being kept in the dark for a month. Roman emperors and French kings used the same practice on the tiny birds: disorientated by the darkness, they eat for 24 hours a day. Once the ortolan has been fattened to bursting point, it is drowned in Armagnac, the brandy that is another speciality of the region.

The bird is then plucked and roasted for eight minutes at 190°C (375°F), and served sizzling in its pale yellow fat. The taste is said to be salty, with a delicate flavour to the fat and a richer, more gamey aspect to the liver, kidneys, lungs and heart. It is served at the table in its entirety, bones and all. The diner places a napkin over his head before eating it.

What is the reason for the napkin? There are three reasons, depending on the Frenchman explaining the custom:

1. The napkin captures the aromas and perfumes in the space around you;
2. You do not want God to see you eating this poor, tiny creature;
3. Eating the bird is incredibly messy and you don't want others to see you with juices dripping down your chin.

Ortolan was on the menu for President Mitterrand's last meal, on New Year's Eve 1995 – eight days before he died in a farmhouse in the hamlet of Latche. The president, aware that his days were numbered, requested a gourmand's last supper to send him on his way. He invited 30 friends and family to the dinner and the last supper began with 30 local Marennes oysters. This was followed by foie gras and capon. There was Sauternes and local red wine. Next up, the ortolans.

'It's absolutely delicious: rather crunchy, with the texture and flavour of hazelnuts,' says French food writer François Simon. 'Some people begin with the head, others with the rear end, and there are competing opinions on how best to enjoy them.'

The most mind-blowing recipe

This accolade must go to Alice B. Toklas and her recipe for Haschich Fudge, which appeared in *The Alice B. Toklas Cook Book*, published in 1954.

In the recipe introduction, Toklas described it as 'the food of Paradise – of Baudelaire's Artificial Paradises: it might provide an entertaining refreshment for a Ladies' Bridge Club ... Euphoria and brilliant storms of laughter, ecstatic reveries and extensions of one's personality on several simultaneous planes are to be complacently expected.'

The recipe calls for dates, figs, almonds, peanuts, cinnamon, nutmeg, coriander – and the primary ingredient: 'a bunch of *canibus sativa*'. With butter and sugar, the mix is transformed into fudge and rolled into balls the size of a walnut. 'It should be eaten with care,' Toklas advised her readers. 'Two pieces are quite sufficient.'

She recognised that obtaining the '*canibus*' could present difficulties, though added, 'In the Americas, while often discouraged, its cousin, called *canibus indica*, has been observed in city window boxes. It should be picked and dried as soon as it has gone to seed and while the plant is still green.'

The American publishers were too scared to include the recipe, though the British publishers (Penguin) had no such qualms. Her fudge, or hash brownies, became notorious.

Frogs' legs? I always walk like this.

The French are renowned, and frequently ridiculed, for their custom of eating frogs' legs. The English find the custom revolting, and are usually the ones doing the ridiculing.

But it seems that we were eating the legs long before the French. In 2013 a major archaeological dig in Wiltshire unearthed evidence of the legs being eaten in Britain, 8,000 years before France. The team, which consists of Mesolithic period experts, also found other types of food including salmon and nuts.

David Jacques, from the University of Buckingham, said people living there thousands of years ago were eating a 'Heston Blumenthal-style menu'. He added, 'This is significant for our understanding of the way people were living around 5,000 years before the building of Stonehenge.'

Do we eat horse? Neigh.

'A woman who ate a horse burger ended up in hospital. Her condition was said to be stable.'

—Joke on Twitter following the horsemeat scandal of 2013

The horsemeat scandal of 2013 caused shock in Britain. Traces of horse DNA were found in supermarkets' beef products – with not one single mention of horse on the labels.

Horse is not only eaten in France, where 15 per cent of the French still eat horse steaks, bought from *boucheries chevaline* – specialist horse butchers. It is eaten in China and Japan. It is eaten in Scandinavia. You will find it on the tables of Belgium, while the average Italian devours about a kilo of horse each year. Some 5 million horses are believed to be eaten annually around the world.

And who exported their old horses to be eaten on the Continent? Yes, it was the British. The well-travelled Matthew Fort says that in Verona, every restaurant seems to have a dish of horse … and donkey too, which is more fatty than horse.

Horsemeat is healthy, lean and rich in iron. The meat is sweet and has a good texture. There is the slight taste of game and it is incredibly tender. It is similar in colour to beef and has great character due to its sweetness and acidity. It can be cooked slowly in the style of *boeuf bourguignon*.

It is not knowingly eaten in Britain. In Anglo-Saxon times, like many other meats, horse was part of the diet until Christians decided horse eating was a heathen practice. The Church issued an edict, banning horse as a food. That's when pork became popular and by the 8th century the Christian writer Theodore of Canterbury noted that 'it is not the custom to eat horses'; but excavations of horse bones from that century and the next have shown that the gee-gees were being butchered and their bones chewed.

In the days when the horse was the main form of transport and was used as a labourer in Britain's mines, poor Britons viewed the horse in the same way the French saw it: namely a solid, hardworking beast that would eventually provide a few meals.

In Britain during the Second World War it was not rationed, though butchers required a licence to sell it. One butcher's shop in Yorkshire continued to sell horse right up until the mid-1950s, and the fat was bought by home bakers to make cakes and pastries. Its decline in popularity was due to its association with poverty and the fact that it was eaten largely by a generation that has died out.

The delicate subject of foie gras, by James Martin

By way of introduction, James Martin is a chef and the long-standing presenter of BBC1's Saturday Kitchen. *He's as passionate about cars as he is about food, and he also loves foie gras. It is a highly controversial food and there are those who would like to see it outlawed. For that reason, it has worked its way into the Locked Larder. This is what James told me when I first came across him a few years ago:*

There is one ingredient I desperately want to cook on *Saturday Kitchen* and it is foie gras. But the producers keep telling me, 'You can't. It's politically incorrect.' For heaven's sake, I know it is politically incorrect – but chefs use it; we can't just ignore its buttery, rich, sweet presence in gastronomy.

This French delicacy is the liver of duck or goose which has been specially fattened (it translates as 'fat liver'), and it brings back particularly fond memories for me. I first came across it when I was thirteen years old and went to France with my father, who was a master of wine. He worked in some of the big, famous wine houses, where there were regular banquets and foie gras was always on the menu.

A year later, when I was training at a restaurant in France, foie gras became one of the first dishes I ever cooked, by pan frying it and serving it with a sort of pear chutney. And last week I was in Paris and had foie gras that was served with fig. So it hasn't changed much over the years, except that these days fig seems a more popular accompaniment than pear.

But the way in which it is produced has made it one of the world's most controversial ingredients. In Winchester, where I have a delicatessen, there is a mob of campaigners who have managed to stop the city's restaurants selling foie gras, and my deli is the only place that sells it.

The other day I was in the deli doing a cookery demonstration – with foie gras, as it happens – when suddenly the campaigners pitched up outside and started protesting.

They were waving banners that said things like 'James Martin is scum' and 'Ban this evil trade'. I wanted to put some of the liver on toast and carry it out to them, partly to show them that it is magnificent but also because they looked hungry. My chef said, 'I don't think that's a wise idea.'

By the time it reached eight o'clock, I went outside to have a word with them but they had vanished. They can't have been too hard-core. Either it had got too cold for them, or they had headed home to watch *EastEnders*. Whatever, the case I'm sure the campaigners will be back because I intend to carry on selling foie gras. When people no longer want to buy it, we'll have to stop selling it. Simple as that.

Anyway, I don't know why people moan about it when we live in a land of battery farms. We don't mind going into a supermarket and buying a chicken that is force-fed s**t and tastes like s**t.

Are we living in a nanny state? We are being dictated to; being told what we can and cannot eat. 'You can do this, you can't do that, you've got to p**s in that direction.' For Christ's sake, it's ridiculous. We must accept that people have a right to choice. If they want to eat fattened goose liver then let them eat it. Who are you to tell them otherwise?

Mind you, I nearly forgot that the worst meal of my life involved foie gras. It was at a three-Michelin-starred restaurant in France and the chef was out to impress my companions. For starters, he served scallops that were the size of footballs; so big you couldn't eat the bloody things. The main course was seared foie gras. Usually it is about 1cm thick maximum. This was about an inch thick. It was the size of a fillet steak and was plonked on top of buttered noodles. It was a laxative in a bowl. I was so sick that night.

For those of you who love it, foie gras comes in tins (pre-cooked) and packets and it freezes well. It is easy to cook. Traditionally, it is pan fried in foaming butter. A lot of people get it wrong because they cook it too slowly. The secret is not to overcook it. Put it into the hot pan, quickly colour it and then remove it. If it's in the pan too long, it'll turn to mush. Classically, it is served on sweet brioche, but I love it on toast. It can be served with fresh figs which are grilled or pan fried, or with fig chutney (it works well with most fruit chutneys).

Then there is foie gras terrine. Step one: Soak the livers overnight in water so that they become slightly soft. Step two: The following day, remove the veins from the livers. Step three: Lay the livers on an oven tray, pour over them a glass of Madeira, add salt and pepper and then roast in the oven at 190°C (375°F) for about eight minutes. Step four: In a terrine, make layers out of cooked chicken and foie gras.

My New Year's resolution is to make the terrine on *Saturday Kitchen*. And then I'll come out of the studio to find someone's chucked red paint over my car!

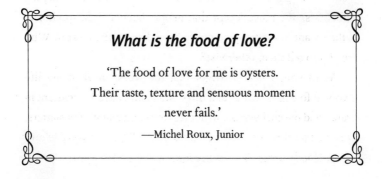

What is the food of love?

'The food of love for me is oysters.
Their taste, texture and sensuous moment
never fails.'

—Michel Roux, Junior

13. THE WINE RACK AND DRINKS TROLLEY

....

Floydy and Blanc and
the subject of cooking with wine

In September 2007, I met Keith Floyd and said, 'I'll take you any-where for lunch. Where would you like to go?'

Keith said he would like to go to Le Manoir aux Quat' Saisons, the restaurant-hotel of Raymond Blanc. We went and, after lunch, Raymond joined us. There followed a conversation about which wine was best to use in coq au vin.

Keith said he would most certainly use Gevrey Chambertin. Prices for this Burgundy start at about £20 a bottle. Raymond was of the opinion that the best wine was a good plonk from Langue-doc costing about a fiver a bottle. Keith challenged Raymond to a cook-off, which never took place. Two years later to the day, Keith died at his partner Celia Martin's home in Dorset.

It really is worthwhile examining this conundrum, which is not the concern of pairing wine with food, but rather knowing which wines should be used in cooking. From my experience, Raymond is right. Even though coq au vin is strongly associated with the region of Burgundy, the wine Burgundy is not a good one to heat up.

France is a mass of regions defined not only geographically but also by strong and specific food and wine traditions. If you happen to live in Bordeaux, you believe that Bordeaux produces the finest cheese and wine. The prejudice is so strong you do not go elsewhere for these products. At some point, coq au vin was established as a dish that was invented in Burgundy, and therefore the people of Burgundy are convinced it should be cooked with a wine from Burgundy. Many cooks and connoisseurs are equally convinced.

However, when you think about it, this dish is really chicken stew made with wine. It is a rustic dish that has been made in every French region.

GOLDEN RULE: never use a great wine to make a dish.

In his memoir *A Taste of My Life*, Raymond writes:

> Before even cooking with wine, we should ask, why use it in the first place? We use it as a marinade, to produce extra flavour with more length, flavours that linger for longer on the palate. Like the juice of lemon, orange or grapefruit, wine is a catalyst of flavour and it is there to make the flavour last, to grow the flavour. It also tenderizes the meat and adds a dramatic colour. Coq au vin has four main elements – chicken, wine, vegetables and herbs – each of which is as important as the other. The chicken brings proteins, flavour and its distinct character. The vegetables and herbs (bay leaf and thyme) impart their own flavours (and never forget garlic, which you find in most French cooking, thank God). Then there is the wine, which not only provides that length of flavour in the finished dish but also the moisture for the cooking process.

What makes Champagne bubbly?

The Foodie's food scientist friend Professor Bob says: 'Champagne has a second fermentation occurring in the bottle. Yeast will produce carbon dioxide, which gives the Champagne its sparkle. The bubbles form on the side of the glass at small imperfections which act as nucleation points – this is why Champagne can sometimes fizz up more in one glass than another.'

From water to wine

About 25 centuries ago, the Greek physician Hippocrates came up with the first water filter. It was made of cloth, conical in shape and was known as *manicum hippocraticum*, that is, Hippocratic sleeve.

Some genius with a taste for alcohol took it one stage further. He mixed wine with sugar and spices, steeped them, and then strained them through the Hippocrates water filter. Ta-dah! The result was 'hippocras' – a bit like mulled wine but unheated.

My historian friend Andrea Zuvich, an expert in 17th-century history, says, 'I make the drink every winter, as the spices are perfect for a winter's night. I use the advice of 17th-century "Hus-Wife" Gervase Markham [of whom more in chapter 14] ...'

To make hippocras (first recipe) –
'To make hippocras, take a bottle of wine, two ounces of good cinnamon, half an ounce of ginger, nine cloves, and six pepper corns, and a nutmeg, and bruise them and put them into the wine with some rosemary flowers, and so let them steep all night, and then put in sugar a pound for that purpose: thus if your wine be claret, the hippocras will be red, if white, then of that colour also.'

To make hippocras (second recipe) –
'Take a gallon of claret or white wine, and put therein four ounces of ginger, an ounce and a half of nutmegs, of cloves one quarter, of sugar four pound; let all this stand together in a pot at least

twelve hours, then take it, and put it into a clean bag made for the purpose, so that the wine may come with good leisure from the spices.'

The oldest wine cellar

Archaeologists in 2013 uncovered a 3,700-year-old wine cellar in the ruins of a Canaanite palace in Israel, and chemical analysis revealed the sophistication of the period's wine-making techniques. Samples from the ceramic jars suggest that they held a luxurious beverage evidently reserved for banquets, researchers said. 'It's not wine that somebody is just going to come home from a hard day and kick back and drink,' said Andrew Koh of Brandeis University. He found signs of a blend of ingredients that may have included honey, mint, cedar, tree resins and cinnamon bark.

The wine of prisoners

Gorgona is a wine made with the help of prisoners on the Tuscan island of Gorgona. Lamberto Frescobaldi – as in the Frescobaldi family, which has been making wine in Italy for over 700 years – wanted to provide 'the inmates with the opportunity of learning winemaking techniques and job skills under the supervision of the company's agronomists and winemakers'. The prison had a small vineyard and wanted to do something with it so it started calling some of the big wine families in Italy. And Frescobaldi says he 'answered the phone', and that's how their participation began. Some 50 inmates worked on the white wine, made from Vermentino and Ansonica grapes that are planted on Gorgona. They only made 2,700 bottles, about a third of them sent to the US market.

What to know about wine

Richard Siddle is the esteemed editor of *Harper's Wine & Spirit*, the publication for those who earn a living from the trade of wine and spirits, be they merchants or sommeliers. I asked Richard to help me out.

Foodie: Can you tell us about the history of wine in about one hundred words, please?

Richard: Well wine is another to add to the list of 'What have the Romans ever done for us'. Wherever the Romans went you can bet there will be a healthy and mostly wealthy wine industry left behind. As to who actually started making wine then there is a lot of competitive bidding going on between the Moldovans, the Georgians, the Lebanese and even the Turks. Take your pick really as they all have a good story to tell. Even though they have been resting a little on their laurels when it comes to the actual quality and volume of wine they have produced ever since.

Foodie: Does wine compare to any other interest?

Richard: Wine is a bit like Formula 1 – or golf, for that matter. You can just enjoy it for what it is. A quick, easy way to enjoy yourself, pass the time of day. Or you can get obsessed with it. Try and know and understand every last little fact about it. But you never will as it is like trying to get your head round the complexities of space, the universe and the meaning of life. Make mine a nice glass of Albariño or Malbec and leave it at that.

Foodie: What is life like for a winemaker?

Richard: A bit like being a posh farmer, really. You get to live in a big house in the middle of nowhere surrounded by fields. But instead of mucking out pigs and hanging out at the stables you get to show off your wines in Michelin-starred restaurants and get told you are a genius by highly impressionable wine writers for picking grapes, sticking them in a fermentation tank and then putting a funny name on the label.

Foodie: In my dreams I own a vineyard. Is this wise?

Richard: Finance. There is an old adage in the wine world that to make a small fortune in wine, you need to start with a large fortune. But don't feel too badly for anyone who tells you that because they are normally stinking rich and fly around the world with a big smile on their face, drinking their expensive wine in wonderful restaurants in beautiful locations.

Foodie: What about investing in wine?

Richard: On the face of it incredibly complicated, with spreadsheets, mile after mile of complex tasting notes and a whole line-up of wine experts willing to charm and confuse you at the same time. On the other hand, it is incredibly easy. Buy wine from certain Bordeaux, Burgundy and Tuscany wine producers you can pick out in seconds on Google. Preferably from a year (or so-called vintage) that is deemed to have been better than others. Ignore everything else.

Foodie: My readers and I would like to pass ourselves off as wine experts. Any tips?

Richard: First, buy a pair of coloured chinos. Preferably red. Get yourself a tweed or sporting jacket. Pop along to Berry Bros & Rudd on St James's Street in London. Buy something you can show off easily and cheaply. A Berry Bros diary or calendar perhaps, and then leave it somewhere in your house where friends and family will see it. The same trick applies to a subscription to wine magazine *Decanter*. When it arrives, bend back a couple of pages and leave it on the coffee table in the front room. You can then go on and actually buy some wine, but without the above you will just be like anyone else.

Foodie: Thank you. That's helpful. What about tasting wine?
Richard: The secret is not to actually drink the wine at all.

Foodie: I beg your pardon.
Richard: At least not for an interminably long time. First you have to swill it around and smell it. And then try to work out what all those alcoholic vapours remind you of. If you said something along the lines of fruit, be it dark or red, then you will be halfway home. Then put the wine in your mouth. If the sides of your mouth start salivating for no particular reason then you can say it is 'acidic'. If it feels like you have put the equivalent of liquid chalk in your mouth then it has probably got a lot of 'tannins' in it. Equally, if it all feels rather wonderful and sits on your tongue just waiting to be transported down your throat then you can say it is 'balanced'.

Foodie: What about tasting wine when a sommelier pours it in a restaurant?
Richard: The only thing to know here is that they are actually not asking you if you like it, but, incredibly, whether you think it is off or not. Even though the sommelier who is asking you has given up much of his youth to know things you will never even dream of or want to know, he needs you to tell him or her that what they have opened is okay to drink. Strange but true. Other wine careers are available. Oh, and you can tell if the wine is not okay to drink if it

smells a bit like the boot of your car if you have left a wet coat in there all weekend.

Foodie: What is the difference between sparkling wine and Champagne?

Richard: About £20 to £30 usually. Other than prestige, how it makes you feel and other than the really tip-top Champagnes, you can save a lot of money and not go too far wrong with a good sparkling wine. Okay, the way it is made is different and the grape varieties they use are different, but they both come out fizzy and refreshing. That said if you like your fizz tasting of honey and biscuits then it is worth splashing out that bit extra for a quality Champagne. Especially on a first date or if you are going to propose.

What wines to drink from where

Stick to this guide and you should not get too embarrassed. There are a few clever clogs tips thrown in for good measure.

Argentina
Red: Malbec
Clever clogs tip: Bonarda (used a lot in blended Argentine wine but set to go it alone more).

White: Torrentes.
Clever clogs tip: Buy white wines from the high up (or in wine terms cool-climate) regions like Salta.

Australia
Red: Shiraz
Clever clogs tip: Big blended wines with the likes of Cabernet

Sauvignon and Shiraz blended with French numbers like Mourvedre, Carignan, Petit Verdot.

White: Chardonnay.

Chile
Red: Carmenere.
Clever clogs tip: Pinot Noir from the regions right on the coast (Colchagua, for one).

White: Sauvignon Blanc.
Clever clogs tip: Look for Rieslings from those high up, cool-climate regions again.

France
Stay local. Buy wines from the region you are in (be hard to do anything else).
Clever clogs tip: Ask for grower wines, that is, small-scale wine producers looking to hit the big time.

(Champagne)
Clever clogs tip: Go for premium own-label lines like Tesco Finest; ask for Champagnes from growers who offer good-quality and good-value Champagnes.

Spain
Red: Tempranillo.
Whites from Ribera del Duero.
Clever clogs tip: Albarino for whites closely followed by the likes of Verdejo and Godello.

Italy

Red: Sangiovese

White: Pinot Grigio

Clever clogs tip: For reds and whites, look for wines from Sicily like Fiano (white) and Nero D'Avola (red).

Portugal

Red: Touriga Nacional.

White: Vinho Verde region.

Clever clogs tip: Check out the big red blends from Douro valley, and whites from Alentejo.

South Africa

Red: Pinotage.

White: Chenin Blanc.

Clever clogs tip: Ask for wine from one of the trendy Swaartland winemakers.

United States

Red: Zinfandel.

White: Chardonnay.

New Zealand

Red: Pinot Noir.

White: Sauvignon Blanc.

Clever clogs tip: Ask for Pinot Noirs from Martinborough or *Jurassic Park* actor Sam Neill's winery in Central Otago, Two Paddocks.

Passing the port

When sharing port, the bottle should be passed around the table, to the left. There are many suggestions for this custom and I have spent many years drinking many bottles of port in an effort to establish which one might be correct. I have settled on this: the decanter is quite heavy and, as we are mostly right-handed, it is polite to pass to the left so that your companion can pick up the bottle with his strongest arm.

Do not feel obliged to follow the custom of drinking port from a small glass. We need our noses to assist our palates – a decent-sized wine glass enables the bouquet of the port to be savoured.

> Sambuca should be served neat with three
> coffee beans – to represent the Holy Trinity.

How to stop a whisky bore

Point out that well-known whisky drinkers include Prince Charles (and, it is said, Camilla), Dylan Thomas, Winston Churchill, Ernest Hemingway, Franklin D. Roosevelt, and then rattle off the English 'translations' of malt whisky distilleries:

Ardberg – 'small headland'
Bruichladdich – 'the bank of the shore'
Bunnahabhain – 'foot or bottom of the river'
Caol Ila – 'narrow island sound'
Laphroaig – 'beautiful hollow by the broad bay'
Glenmorangie – 'valley of peace'

The men behind the blends

Is it easier to remember the names of blended whiskies, rather than the single malts? Definitely. Bell's, which is the UK's most successful whisky, was the brainchild of Arthur Bell in the 19th century.

Teacher's was created by William Teacher in the 1860s.

Johnnie Walker began his spirits business selling whisky from his grocery store in Ayrshire, Scotland. His whiskies were very popular and, following his death in 1857, the company was passed down to his son, Alexander Walker. Alexander, with the help of his son, also called Alexander, established the brand and greatly increased its popularity. The first blend – Walker's Old Highland – was created in 1865. The rectangular bottle was introduced in 1870. During the early 20th century, Alexander Walker II and George Walker, Johnnie's grandsons, established the colour naming system.

In 1908, the Johnnie Walker name was introduced to the product when the managing director, James Stevenson, rebranded the range. The walking figure was also conceived around this time. Today, there is a good range: Red, the international best-selling Scotch blend; Black, Swing, Green, Gold and the premium Blue label.

So whereas a romantic, unpronounceable name equals a malt, a person's name equals a blended whisky.

Hangovers

Friends and family may call you an idiot. A hangover is Mother Nature's way of saying it.

It is believed that if you drink too much alcohol then you will always suffer the disagreeable after-effects. This is not true. Beer and spirits, maybe. However, a surplus of good wine does not tend to cause a hangover.

Cures for the hangover include:

Milk thistle. Protects liver cells from toxins and should be taken before consumption of alcohol.

A fry-up. Many British people who are feeling sick believe that there is only one cure for the alcohol-induced nausea: to eat a plate that is piled high with greasy fried eggs, sausages, bacon, black pudding, white pudding, haggis, baked beans and fried bread, garnished with condiments of tomato ketchup and Daddies Sauce. It sounds good on paper ... actually, it doesn't even sound good on paper.

Prairie oyster. 1 raw egg, 1 tsp Worcestershire sauce, pinch of salt, pepper, 2 dashes of Tabasco sauce. Crack the egg into a glass, leaving the yolk unbroken. Douse it with Worcestershire sauce, a sprinkling of salt and pepper, and Tabasco sauce. Knock it back in one. And one is all you need because once you've had one slimy prairie oyster you will never have another. It will make you feel sick.

Drink lots of water. Boring. Watch it, though. Drink can kill, and that includes drinking too much water. There's a condition known as hyponatraemia, which is usually associated with ecstasy takers and marathon runners and often mistaken for heat exhaustion. Water dilutes the body's salt and leads to symptoms that can be fatal: headaches, weakness, nausea, confusion, unsteadiness, agitation, delirium, unconsciousness ... death. Most big drinkers don't drink much water so they are not in great danger.

Hair of the dog. The premise is that like cures like, which is nonsense when it comes to alcohol. This 'cure' involves the risk of getting drunk again, which is simply delaying an even mightier hangover. But it sounds promising and has romantic roots. The expression originally referred to a method of treating a dog bite – placing a hair from the dog on the wound to heal it – which, of course, it wouldn't.

Ebenezer Cobham Brewer writes in the *Dictionary of Phrase and Fable* (1898): 'In Scotland it is a popular belief that a few hairs of the dog that bit you applied to the wound will prevent evil consequences. Applied to drinks, it means, if overnight you have indulged too freely, take a glass of the same wine within 24 hours to soothe the nerves. "If this dog do you bite, soon as out of your bed, take a hair of the tail the next day."'

He also cites two apocryphal poems containing the phrase, one of which is attributed to Aristophanes. It is possible that the phrase was used to justify an existing practice, and the idea of *similia similibus curantur* (that 'like cures like') dates back at least to the time of Hippocrates.

If you are feeling jaded and a Hungarian tells you 'kutya-harapást szőrével', do not be offended – it simply means you may cure 'the dog's bite with its fur' and the Hungarian is trying to be helpful.

The Amis novelists on hangovers

The subject of the hangover is neatly handled in British litera-ture by Kingsley Amis and his son Martin Amis. In fact, Martin described his father as 'the laureate of the hangover'.

Below: compare and contrast these two passages.

From *Lucky Jim* by Kingsley Amis:

Dixon was alive again. Consciousness was upon him before he could get out of the way; not for him the slow, gracious wandering from the halls of sleep, but a summary, forcible ejection. He lay sprawled, too wicked to move, spewed up like a broken spider-crab on the tarry shingle of morning. The light did him harm, but not as much as looking at things did; he resolved, having done it once, never to move his eye-balls again. A dusty thudding in his head made the scene before him beat like a pulse. His mouth had been used as a latrine by some small creature of the night, and then as its mausoleum. During the night, too, he'd somehow been on a cross-country run and then been expertly beaten up by secret police. He felt bad.

From *The Information* by Martin Amis:

Just as there are genres of skies, and car alarms, and many other things, so there are genres of the hangover …

At first it seemed that Richard's hangover might find a relatively comfortable generic home: the country-house mystery. Every hangover, after all, is a mystery; every hangover is a whodunit. But as soon as he reared and swivelled from his bed, and placed a plumply quivering white sole on the lino, it was amply and dreadfully clear what genre he was in: horror. This horror was irresponsibly absolute, yet also low-budget: cheaply dubbed, ill-lit, and hand-held …

There was a mirror, above the washbasin: Richard went and stared at the gormless ghoul who lived behind the glass. Such hair as had not fallen out overnight now stood on end, and his mouth was crinkled like a frozen chip. Nor did he not perceive that he had another black eye.

The Foodie's hangover cure:
perchance the world's greatest remedy

Once again, logic is applied. In order to find the best remedy for a hangover, go to the place where the hangovers are worst. That is the Caribbean, the West Indies and any island where cheap rum is drunk in vast quantities. The hangovers there are horrendous. Or rather, they would be. How do the inhabitants avoid illness the morning after? They smile. But think of the diet, which includes bananas and coconuts – the inspiration for the Foodie's hangover cure. Coconut water is rich in potassium and rehydrates the body, while banana raises blood sugar levels. Both ingredients boost the spirits.

Ingredients:
1 banana
200ml (7fl oz) coconut water
100ml (3½fl oz) whole milk
50ml (2fl oz) double cream
Juice of 1 lime

Method:
Insert earplugs.

In a blender or using a stick blender, blitz all ingredients to a smooth liquid and drink.

Women and wine

The American organisation A Woman's Palate aims to promote women vintners, share their wines with a larger audience of women and educate women about wine in general.

A 2010 Gallup poll found that 48 per cent of women who drink prefer wine, compared with 17 per cent of men. Wine-tasting groups among women are on the increase, and wine merchants have made varied attempts to market directly to women. Some wineries have even created wines specifically targeted at female drinkers such as 'Little Black Dress', 'Girly Girl' and 'Bitch', although the names alone would put off any serious student of the grape.

A Woman's Palate recognises the growing importance of wine, and that, as more women advance into the executive ranks and are expected to entertain, they want to know how to order wine for professional reasons as well as personal enjoyment.

Don't buy fake

Be careful! In 2013, French police busted a scam in which merchants made £2 million selling fake bottles of an expensive vintage wine across Europe. The bottles of poor-quality wine were allegedly re-labelled as the Burgundy red Romanée-Conti, with counterfeit labels. The labels were treated with wax to make them look older. In 2011, a twelve-bottle case of the real thing, dating back to 1990, sold for £200,000 at auction.

Turning your home into a winery

Grapes produce great wine but it's all rather predictable. Instead, you can make wine at home from the following:

Beetroot: Can take a year to be ready to drink.

Nettles: Young leaves can be made into beer or wine, but avoid older leaves as they contain inorganic crystals – not good for your kidneys!

Parsnip: Add ripe banana for perfect balance.

Pears: Infuse herbs, such as basil or rosemary, for extra flavour.

Plums: Ready within a few months.

Silver birch: Mmm. Wine from a tree? Tap the tree when the sap's sweetness is at its height (usually March) for a light, mineral wine.

Wines can also be made from chilli, lavender, lemon balm and rhubarb.

The birth of AA

In the summer of 1935 a stockbroker called Bill visited Akron, Ohio, on a business trip. There he met a doctor called Bob and shared with him his experiences as an alcoholic and his method of recovery from the disease of alcoholism. It would be nice to say he shared his experiences 'over drinks', but there were no alcoholic drinks.

Doctor Bob was intrigued because he was also an alcoholic and, in fact, he was suffering an almighty hangover at the time. Bob had the last alcoholic drink of his life.

The following day, 11 June, the two men founded what is now known as Alcoholics Anonymous. The fellowship, which is founded on the concept of alcoholics helping one another on the steps to recovery, has a presence in 170 countries and has had millions of members. It's known for optimistic, memorable, medicinal catchphrases such as 'one day at a time' and 'an alcoholic is an egomaniac with an inferiority complex', and the line (attributed to the late Irish writer Brendan Behan) '[For me] one drink is too many, and a thousand not enough.'

14. THE VEGETABLE RACK

Salads of the 17th century

The Foodie's friend Andrea Zuvich is an expert on the 17th century. Aside from having an expansive knowledge, she takes part in re-enactments and has written two historical novels set in the 1800s. Here, she writes a few words ...

The 17th century was in many ways a turning point in the history of food. In general, changes in food habits were gradual, and at the beginning of the 17th century, Tudor fare was still very much the standard. With better trade routes going farther than ever before, new and interesting foods, beverages and food customs were introduced. Ale during the Tudor period was darker, malty, but after the Glorious Revolution and with the Dutch influence, beer was made with more hops and tastes changed.

The most useful book on running an early 17th-century home was written by Gervase Markham and is entitled, *The English Hus-Wife* [Housewife]: *containing, The inward and outward vertues which ought to be in a Compleat woman*. This book, published in 1615, is a wonderfully rich source of information on a variety of topics associated with maintaining the day-to-day workings of a household.

Sallats (salads) became increasingly popular, and these colourful dishes were often found in recipe books of the time. Markham includes several recipes for salads in *The English Housewife*, but even celebrated diarist John Evelyn was so fond of them that he wrote *Acetaria: A Discourse of Sallets*.

One salad example from Markham is the following:

An excellent boiled sallat

To make an excellent compound boiled sallat: take of spinach well washed two or three handfuls, and put it into fair water, and boil it till it be exceeding soft, and tender as pap; then put it into a colander and drain the water from it: which done, with the backside of your chopping knife to chop it, and bruise it as small as may be: then put it into a pipkin with a good lump of sweet butter, and boil it over again; then take a good handful of currants clean washed, and put to it, and stir them well together; then put to as much vinegar as will make it reasonable tart, and then with sugar season it according to the taste of the master of the house.

Dressing for a salad

The classic dressing for salad is simple enough to make. It is merely the combination of oil and vinegar. Heavens! It sounds simple but can all go wrong. The two can be mixed, of course, but will soon separate. Water (which is a component of vinegar) and oil don't mix. To enable them to mix, a teaspoon of mustard is first whisked in the oil. The mustard is a bonding agent, preventing the separation of oil and vinegar. (For the same reason, mustard is an ingredient of mayonnaise.) A multitude of ingredients – salt, pepper, herbs, spices – can be added to the basic vinaigrette to alter or enhance its flavour.

The fashionable salad maker

Those who cannot be bothered to make it can buy salad dressings from supermarkets.

The Victorians in London did not know such convenience. They could not despatch an order to Ocado and then await a text: 'Derek will be making your Ocado delivery in his onion horse and carriage.' Ocado, you see, did not exist.

Instead, wealthy Victorians who lived in London sent for a man known as the Fashionable Salad Maker. He was a Frenchman, named d'Albignac (or d'Aubignac), who was born and raised in Limousin, and finally pitched up in London, though with very little money after the Napoleonic Wars. Being a Frenchman he decided to spend what money he had on food and visited what was one of the earliest restaurants in London. He was excitedly discussing a piece of roast beef and, sitting on a table beside him, were five or six dandies. One of them said, 'Sir, they say your people excel in the art of making a salad. Will you be kind enough to oblige us?'

D'Albignac agreed, and there and then created a salad of divine taste, texture and flavour. One of the dandies handed him a tenner, and d'Albignac gave them his address. Shortly afterwards he was surprised to receive an invitation to dress a salad at one of the best houses in Grosvenor Square.

Brillat-Savarin recounts in *The Physiology of Taste* (the gourmet's bible) what happened next:

> D'Albignac began to see that he might draw considerable benefit from it, and did not hesitate to accept the offer. He took with him various preparations which he fancied would

make his salad perfect as possible. He took more pains in this second effort, and succeeded better than he had at first. On this occasion so large a sum was handed to him that he could not with justice to himself refuse to accept it. The young men he met first, had exaggerated the salad he had prepared for them, and the second entertainment was yet louder in its praise.

D'Albignac, like a man of sense, took advantage of the excitement, and soon obtained a carriage, that he might travel more rapidly from one part of the town to the other. He had in a mahogany case all the ingredients he required [caviar, truffles, anchovies, ketchup, aromatic flavourings].

Subsequently he had similar cases prepared and filled, which he used to sell by the hundred. Ultimately he made a fortune of 80,000 francs, which he took to France when times became more peaceful.

Brillat-Savarin observes that d'Albignac purchased a small estate, 'on which, for aught I know, he now lives happily'.

On the subject of calories

What exactly is a calorie and how is one measured?
The calorie is a unit of measurement of energy. Most consumers are actually interested in kilocalories or 'Calories' with a capital 'C'. Traditionally the energy content of a food was determined by burning it and measuring the heat liberated as a result. Nowadays we already know the energy content of the basic components of food and so the calorie content of a specific product is determined by adding up the contribution of all of the ingredients.

Jackie Kennedy liked her lunch to have no more than 500 calories

Frequently, her lunch consisted of a large baked potato (150 calories), split and heaped with a spoonful of fresh caviar (100 calories). With this she would drink a glass of Champagne (100 calories). And then maybe another glass of Champagne (100 calories). Total: 450 calories.

It's a myth ...

... that you use more calories eating raw celery than are contained in the celery, but if you want to eat foods with even fewer calories per 100g try lettuce (13 calories), cooked cabbage (14 calories), or fresh Jerusalem artichoke (7 calories). Personally, I prefer lots of calories so try to eat at least 100g of walnuts per day – this provides me with 654 calories.

A bit more about walnuts

In 2011 scientific studies showed that walnuts contain the highest level of antioxidants compared to other nuts. Antioxidants are known to help protect the body against disease: they stop the chain reactions that damage cells in the body when oxidation occurs.

People who smoke and drink like trenchermen should eat walnuts in order to extend their lives. The scientists didn't say that. It's just my opinion but it makes sense.

The scientists said that all nuts have good nutritional qualities but walnuts are healthier than peanuts, almonds, pecans and pistachios. Dr Joe Vinson, from the University of Scranton, analysed the antioxidant levels of nine different types of nuts and discovered that a handful of walnuts contained twice as many antioxidants as a handful of any other commonly eaten nut.

He found that these antioxidants were higher in quality and potency than in any other nut.

The antioxidants found in walnuts were also two to fifteen times as powerful as vitamin E, which is known to protect the body against damaging natural chemicals involved in causing disease, the study says. Nuts are known to be healthy and nutritious, containing high-quality protein, lots of vitamins and minerals as well as dietary fibre. They are also dairy- and gluten-free.

Previous research has shown that regular consumption of small amounts of nuts can reduce the risk of heart disease, some types of cancer, type two diabetes and other health problems. Dr Vinson said there was another advantage in choosing walnuts as a source of antioxidants: 'The heat from roasting nuts generally reduces the quality of the antioxidants. People usually eat walnuts raw or unroasted, and get the full effectiveness of those antioxidants.'

Getting back to vegetables, as this is the veg chapter, here's a story about carrots.

Carrots and the battle to get us to eat them

John Cunningham was an RAF pilot who became a national hero during the Second World War because of his skill at shooting down enemy bombers during night raids over Britain. He notched up 20 kills and earned the nickname 'Cat's Eyes' because of his incredible night vision. The Royal Air Force said that Cunningham – and his co-fighters in the RAF – were exceptional because of one thing – carrots. The carrots helped the pilots see in the dark.

It was propaganda gone mad. The British didn't want the Germans to know of their real secret weapon: the recently invented on-board radar system.

This ruse coincided with a glut in carrots, of which the Government was aware. It was keen for people to eat as much as possible of the vegetable. There were 500,000 tons to get through!

Incidentally, carrots don't really help us see in the dark. The orange colours in carrots (carotenes) can be metabolised into vitamin A in the body but this will not improve vision in a healthy individual. They might help prevent problems with vision developing in individuals who are vitamin A deficient.

The Smith recipe for a salad dressing

The writer, wit and gourmet Sydney Smith (1771–1845) was particular when it came to making a salad dressing. He advised:

> Take care not to use that excessively pungent and deleterious combination of drugs which is now so frequently imposed upon the public, as the best white wine vinegar. In reality, it has no vinous material about it, and it may be known by its violent and disagreeable sharpness, which overpowers and destroys the taste (and also the substance) of whatever it is mixed with. And it is also very unwholesome. Its colour is always very pale, and it is nearly as clear as water. No one should buy or use it. The first quality of real cider vinegar is good for all purposes.

Here is his enchanting poem, an ode to the salad dressing.

> To make this condiment your poet begs
> The pounded yellow of two hard-boil'd eggs;
> Two boiled potatoes, passed through kitchen sieve,
> Smoothness and softness to the salad give.

Let onion atoms lurk within the bowl,
And, half-suspected, animate the whole.
Of mordant mustard add a single spoon,
Distrust the condiment that bites so soon;
But deem it not, thou man of herbs, a fault
To add a double quantity of salt;
Four times the spoon with oil of Lucca crown,
And twice with vinegar procur'd from town;
And lastly o'er the flavour'd compound toss
A magic soupçon of anchovy sauce.
Oh, green and glorious! Oh, herbaceous treat!
Twould tempt the dying anchorite to eat;
Back to the world he'd turn his fleeting soul,
And plunge his fingers in the salad-bowl!
Serenely full, the epicure would say,
'Fate cannot harm me, I have dined today.'

> Did you know that between 2011 and 2013 the amount of people buying sweet potatoes in the UK has gone up by 34 per cent? Am I kidding myself? Of course, you didn't know that. Why should you? A sweet potato isn't actually a potato at all. It is a vegetable and part of the morning glory family of flowering plants. These potatoes-that-aren't-potatoes can also be eaten raw, and are a welcome addition when grated into salads or coleslaw.

The potato

Is this the most versatile of vegetables, even if it is a tuber?

It was not introduced to Britain by Sir Walter Raleigh. That's a myth. The pomme (the 'de terre' is deleted in kitchen speak) can be prepared in hundreds of different ways – just thinking of the ways that begin with an 'A' …

À **l'Albufera:** cut into ball shapes, parboiled and simmered in Albufera sauce.

Alsacienne: large, nut-shaped boiled potatoes, served with fried, chopped onions and with parsley sprinkled over.

Anna: thin sliced potatoes (as chips) baked in a mould, or casserole, with butter until brown.

Annette: as Anna, but with chopped onions and cheese added.

Ardennaise: baked then scooped; potato mixed with purée of chicken, ham and mixed herbs then placed in the potato skin and browned under a grill.

Au four: baked with bacon fat and onion.

Moving through the alphabet, there's pommes Bengal (mashed potatoes mixed with Bengal chutney and lightly browned), pommes Robert (mashed, mixed with chives and mixed herbs) and pommes Vauban, which is simply diced potatoes fried in olive oil.

On garlic

Ideally, garlic should be peeled and then sliced or crushed at least ten minutes before cooking. This process enables the enzymes to start work, so that they impart optimum health benefits in the dish. What are these health benefits? Garlic boosts the immune system in chilly weather, strengthens it generally and reduces the risk of heart attack. It is also widely believed to cure impotency. But garlic is also rich in Vitamin B, which makes us feel happy. A garlicky dish of pasta is a cure for the blues.

Years ago I was told that garlic and onion should never be added at the same time to a dish, and that the Italians have a saying along the lines, 'Garlic and onion marry well but can't go into church at the same time.' Now I can't find any Italians to corroborate this adage, and my Italian friends are avoiding me. Nonetheless, it does appear that to add garlic and onion at the same time affects the flavour of the dish – one seems to overpower the other.

On the prevention of tears when slicing onions

Onions (which, incidentally, should not be stored beside potatoes as each affects the other's freshness) release an odour when sliced. It makes the slicer cry.

To prevent crying, there are several suggested remedies. These include wearing goggles designed for skiing or swimming, and placing in the mouth a large slice of bread.

I would recommend one of the following two options:

1. Learn to slice an onion very quickly, keeping the root on the onion when slicing.
2. Cut the onion in half and place it in the freezer for 15–30 minutes. Remove from freezer and slice.

When making a ragu or a bolognaise sauce, it pays to use a food processor to cut up onions and use lots of them. Why? Because there is a chemical compound in onions that enhances meaty flavours, called MMP (3-mercapto-2-methylpentan). It is released in abundance when you cut onions, especially finely, and especially in a food processor. The sulphur compound, when heated, tastes very meaty so the more you can create the better. Adding water as you sweat the onions also helps, as it is a water-soluble compound.

The perfect roast potatoes

In order to achieve the perfect 'roasties' it's best to think about what happens to the potatoes after they have been par-boiled and before they are popped into the oven.

At this stage, they are hot. The heat has opened the pores of the potatoes. If at this point they are now placed into the roasting tin and straight in the oven (as many chefs recommend) all will be lost. The surface of the potatoes will be swiftly 'sealed' by the heat of the oven.

Instead, the trick is to place the par-boiled potatoes into a cold roasting tin in which there is a generous amount of cold oil. Olive oil, a light Spanish one, is ideal. Leave them to sit in the oil for an hour or so. The oil will then be absorbed by the potato. Once in the oven, the heat will penetrate the potato and perfect crispiness will be accomplished.

Incidentally, the same trick should be used when making potato salad: while the potatoes are still hot, combine them with the mayonnaise and sliced onion so that the flavours are absorbed into the flesh of the potato.

Raw vegetables and the Hemingway diet

When writing, Ernest Hemingway lived on rye crisps, raw, green vegetables and peanut butter sandwiches.

The newspaper *Gazzettino Sera* from 24 March 1954 reported: 'Ernest Hemingway announced he will stay in Venice to recover from the injuries incurred in the well-known African accidents [namely two aeroplane crashes within a week of each other, the second leaving him with first-degree burns, internal bleeding, ruptured kidney, ruptured spleen, ruptured liver, a crushed vertebra and a fractured skull], with a powerful cure based on scampi and *Valpolicella*.' For the writer, this 'diet' was more effective than any kind of powerful medical treatment.

The veg pie that became carnivore's delight

The Cornish pasty is one of the world's most famous meat pies. But it began life – around the 14th century – as strictly vegetarian. Swede, onion and potato were boiled and became the filling of the pie. The meat, shredded, came later along with pasties that had two courses: meat in one end, jam or dried fruit in the other. Hearty and substantial, it was the perfect staple food of tin miners in Cornwall.

A traditional Cornish pasty is D-shaped and has a crimped edge, which looks fancy but is believed to have served a life-saving purpose. Tin mines contained arsenic, which could make its way on to the miners' hands. They held the pie by the crimped edge and then threw away the edge just in case it was contaminated. So a true Cornish pasty must be crimped on the edge and not on the top.

> Red cabbage can lose its redness when simmering. It can turn purple or a worrying blue. Prevent discolouration by adding a couple of teaspoons of vinegar to the water.

Talking fennel with Mary Berry

By way of introduction, the great lady cook and undisputed national (surely global?) treasure Mary Berry is a delight, both on television and in person. As she is the co-presenter of Great British Bake-Off, *you might expect her to feature in the chapter entitled 'The Cake Tin'.*

That would be predictable. Oh all right, she deserves a mention in The Cake Tin, but I recall our chat about fennel. Here are Mary's words on a vegetable that she cherishes.

There are people who claim to hate the taste of fennel. My husband is anti-fennel. In fact, he doesn't like things that his mother didn't cook. If we have people for supper* and I do a fennel dish, he will eat it and say, 'Wasn't that delicious!' But if I put it in front of him, pointed at it and told him it contained fennel, he'd say, 'Oh, but you know I don't like it.' Isn't that typical?

There is a good deal to be said for fennel, which in recent years has become one of my favourites. It seems strange now, but if you go back ten years or so fennel was not readily available. In fact, when I was a child, it was unheard of to use the fennel bulb (and I talk as someone who can remember the days when you couldn't buy avocado in Britain).

Back then, fennel leaves were used as a herb with fish. We had it in our garden, and I remember when Mum was cooking trout she'd cut fennel from huge plants and place it in the belly of the fish before baking it. If you went on holiday to France, there would be fennel on the roadside, growing wild. You ran your hands through it and got this lovely, but very strong aroma.

Now we have the fennel bulb, which I think originally came from France, which is very different. In its raw form, it has a strong

---

* Mary uses the word 'supper'. Should it be 'dinner' or 'supper'? Dinner is considered to be the main meal of the day and originally began at what we now know as lunchtime. 'Supper' stems from the French *soper*, meaning to eat the evening meal. From *soper* we not only get 'supper' but also 'sip', 'sop' and 'soup'. It's probably correct to say 'supper', but its use has social repercussions: supper is very much a posh word.

aniseed flavour, and can be tough and chewy. Once it is cooked or marinated, that very strong aniseed flavour diminishes.

I always try to find a big, fat bulb rather than an elongated one as the latter will be less mature. Then I will store it intact in the fridge: if you start pulling the leaves from it, the remaining ones will start to turn brown. Once cut, it will oxidise very quickly and begin to discolour. A bit of lemon juice will prevent discolouration. Failing that, cook with it quickly.

If I'm making a salad, I will use raw fennel but in order to remove that chewy texture I shred it or grate it finely. I drop it into a dressing which contains vinegar or lemon juice (to prevent discolouration). The fennel softens and produces a lovely flavour to the dressing.

But if I am not using it raw, then I have found the best trick is often to boil the fennel first until it is just tender and is no longer stringy.

I do a potato and fennel gratin, which is dead simple and absolutely wonderful. It's a dish that takes into consideration all those people who don't have too much time to cook, but when they do they want to create something delicious in a short period of time.

Step one: Take a couple of fennel bulbs and cut them into wedges and some very large potatoes and also cut them into wedges. Step two: Put the fennel wedges into a large pan of salted water, bring to the boil and simmer for five minutes. Step three: Add the potato wedges and cook for a further five minutes. Step four: Drain the vegetables (at this point, they are not quite cooked), toss them in butter and crushed garlic, and arrange in an open dish and sprinkle with Parmesan. This part of the dish can be done well in advance of serving (the night before or the morning of your dinner party) and as the vegetables are partly cooked they will not discolour. Step five: Half an hour before serving, put the dish into an oven preheated to 180°C (350°F/Gas 4) for about 30 minutes.

I did that dish for a dinner party last New Year's Eve and took it to the house where we were all having a party and popped it in the Aga for the final stage of cooking. Everybody loved it, including the people who would have previously said they don't like fennel.

I also make a fennel, potato and onion soup, which, again, is easy. Step one: Take about 400g (14oz) each of fennel, onion and potato and chop them coarsely. Step two: On a low heat, cook the fennel and onion in butter, so that they caramelise slightly and become tender. Step three: Add the chopped potato, continue to cook until it is also tender and then add about one litre (1¾ pints) of stock. I would use stock cubes (chicken or vegetable) but if you have fresh chicken stock then that would be lovely. Step four: Add a finely chopped chilli and simmer until everything is tender. Season and then liquidise.

Lovers of fish pie should also know that fennel can greatly enhance the flavour. Follow your favourite fish pie recipe, but also try this: Coarsely chop a bulb of fennel and then simmer it in white wine (just enough to cover the top of the fennel) until the vegetable is tender. Then add the fennel to the pie's béchamel sauce. It's a simple addition to a simple dish, but you'll not get a complaint from those guests who insist they can't eat fennel.

Thank you Mary.

What is the food of love?

'My food of love comes from growing up in a
Cuban-Creole and African American household.
A tradition of bold, harmonious flavours went into
a steaming, hot bowl of "Steamed Shellfish Sofrito".
Black mussels, littleneck clams, jumbo prawns and
spicy andouille sausage, all steamed together in a
rich, aromatic Cuban sofrito broth of white wine,
garlic, coriander, tomato, oregano and bell pepper.
This dish is a family favourite and is shared at the
dining room table for all to enjoy and love.'

—Kai Chase, Los Angeles, chef to the stars.

15. THE FISH KETTLE

‘However great the dish that holds the turbot,
the turbot is always greater than the dish.’

—Martial, *Epigrams*

The poaching of the wild salmon

Nothing could be easier. Few cooking ventures are as rewarding.

First, take yourself to a shop and buy a salmon (or some say fish) kettle. It will cost about the same as the wild salmon itself. Both are worthwhile investments, though one will last a great deal longer than the other. Next, go to the fishmonger and buy the wild salmon.

Ask the fishmonger to remove the scales. Otherwise, do this at home, running the blunt side of a knife along the fish. It's messy so place the fish on top of newspaper – or, better, sit it in the bottom of a supermarket plastic bag – before you start with your knife.

Place the salmon in the kettle and fill the kettle with cold water, so that the water just covers the salmon. Add a glass or two of white wine, a few bay leaves and three pinches of salt. Place the kettle on the hob, and over the lowest possible heat: just a flicker of a flame, if you are on gas.

That is it. You are almost done.

When the first bubble appears on the surface of the water – which might take an hour or so – turn off the heat. Allow the salmon to sit in the water for the time it takes to drink one cup of tea or two small glasses of Chablis, whichever is the longest.

Remove the salmon, as 'tis cooked.

When cooking a whole lobster (with a weight of approximately 500g/1lb 2oz) only cook for 3 minutes and then place in a bowl, cover with cling film and allow to steam for about 20 minutes.

Cock crabs and hen crabs at a glance

The claws of cock crabs are similarly sized. Hen crabs have one claw larger than the other. This larger claw is to bash away the over-amorous cock crab. It's no surprise that the word derives from our Viking forefathers, *krabbi* meaning to claw or scratch.

Store fresh fish and shellfish wrapped in newspaper that has been soaked in water.

Jellied eels

Jellied eels were once the staple diet of the working classes. Back in the 18th century there were hundreds of pie makers who wandered the streets of London selling their pies. It was the cheapest form of a shop. No rate, no rent, no taxes.

The eels came from the Thames. And when the Thames became too dirty, the eels came from Holland. They made their way to Billingsgate market and the pie makers would swarm Billingsgate, buy the eels and then make their pies, delicious with mash and parsley liquor. Next came the pie and mash shop, loved by the Victorians, Edwardians and their descendants – one or two shops still remain in London. There, the forks are tied to the table – originally so that customers couldn't steal them. A woman comes along with a bucket of soapy water and cleans the cutlery at the table.

Eat sardines only in months without an 'r' as they are more fatty and delicious.

Some tips about SHELLFISH and FISH

Shells should be firmly closed when buying mussels, cockles and clams. They should smell of the sea. If concerned, simply tap two mussels – if they still don't close, discard.

Herbs that are soft go best with shellfish (and white fish), e.g. tarragon, chervil, parsley, bay leaves and lemon thyme. Capers are great, too.

Enjoy wild salmon from the beginning of June in the UK.

Late August and the beginning of September is the best season for lobster in the UK.

Loosen the beards from mussels by pulling them towards the fat part of the shell, before giving them a tug.

Fish that is oily has its oil stored in its flesh rather than its liver. Cod, hake and turbot are all non-oily; mackerel, salmon and trout are all oily.

It's unwise to eat 'fresh' fish on Mondays – fishermen don't work on Sundays.

Scallops should be hand-dived. The dredged ones are often dead and full of sand, and the dredging process destroys the sea bed.

How to cure or gravlax – or gravadlax – for mathematicians: 1. weigh the fish; 2. divide this figure by four; 3. use the quarter figure to create an equal mix of salt and sugar; 4. add in your desired herbs and aromatics and rub over the fish.

On the subject of prawns by Pascal Proyart

By way of introduction, Pascal Proyart was born and raised in a small fishing village on the Brittany coast, where his family have been restaurateurs for three generations. He has been Executive Chef at One-O-One since June 1998. It is one of the most acclaimed fish restaurants in London. I came across him a few years ago, and said, 'Pascal, we share a mutual love of prawns.' Ever-passionate, he took it from there …

When I first started dating Rosslyn I took her back to Brittany to meet my family. We sat by the seaside with a great big bowl of prawns and as she peeled them I noticed that she would discard the head after pulling it from the body.

This is a big no-no in France. I tried to explain to Rosslyn that while the British chuck away the head, the French devour it because it's the most flavoursome part of the body. Rosslyn said, 'No, no, no. You can't eat it.' But when she tried it, she knew precisely what I meant (and the experience didn't deter her from marrying me).

The French tend to think the British are a bit funny when it comes to prawns. In France, we buy most of our prawns when they are in shells, and we like to think that the peeling process – accompanied by a glass of wine and mayonnaise – encourages good conversation.

In Britain, prawns are mostly bought once they have been shelled and when they are sitting in a pool of water as they defrost in a plastic container on a supermarket shelf. Thing is, the shell is not only attractive in presentation terms, but it also serves a purpose: it keeps the flesh moist. If necessary, it can be removed just before cooking.

One of the best ways to cook prawns is *a la plancha* style: Heat olive oil slowly and then gently fry a generous amount of chopped or crushed garlic (remember, if the heat is too high the garlic will turn black and taste bitter).

When the garlic starts to colour, put in the prawns (leave the head on, remove the shell).

Then add sea salt (I always season prawns during the cooking process, rather than beforehand) and a bit of chopped chilli to add heat and a kick. Finish it with chopped parsley if you want the French touch, or chopped coriander if you want the Asian touch. Then deglaze the pan with lemon juice, and pour these juices over the prawns. Make sure you have a loaf of French bread to soak up the sauce.

Watch the heat when cooking prawns. Some cooks think you throw in the prawns when the pan is smoking hot, and all their guests are left choking and feeling sick. Please, please don't make the heat too aggressive.

My dad used to have a restaurant and he served a lovely dish made with prawns. Each night for about twenty years diners would come in and ask for this dish, which was so simple you could easily do it at home and impress your friends and family. It is absolutely awesome.

To begin with, make garlic butter, using not only butter and garlic, but also shallots, lots of chopped curly leafed parsley, a touch of lemon juice and some cayenne pepper. I also like to add some unsweetened almond powder, which provides a nutty flavour that works well with the prawns.

When the butter mixture is ready, heat olive oil and butter in a pan and fry the prawns (with their heads on, shells off) just to seal them. Then add a touch of brandy, and flambé the prawns. Now add the garlic butter mix and allow it to melt with the prawns, but also making sure the fish does not overcook. Remove the prawns from the pan.

Into the pan add a dash of cream, a squeeze of lemon juice, salt and pepper, stirring it all together before returning the prawns to the pan. Serve with rice and, again, some French bread to mop up the sauce. It's a fantastic dish, and even fussy kids love it.

But I can't talk about the prawn without mentioning the cocktail. Nothing beats the prawn cocktail ...

Firstly, make a mayonnaise. Sure, you can use Hellmann's. But I implore you to make your own because it is delicious and takes just a couple of minutes. Every cookbook has a recipe for mayonnaise (it's egg yolk, rapeseed oil, a bit of mustard and I always add a dash of red wine vinegar at the end).

Once you have made it you have your base for a good sauce. You can add a touch of Worcestershire sauce, some ketchup, cayenne pepper. I always add two other ingredients: lemon juice, because it is the thing that wakes up all the other ingredients; and a dash of good cognac or brandy.

I serve it with a crispy iceberg lettuce or baby gem, chopped vine tomatoes (people talk about summer being the best time for tomatoes, but they are actually best in September and October when they are more mature). I add chopped, hard-boiled eggs, a bit of parsley, a wedge of lemon ... and there you go: prawn cocktail.

For stir-fries, the tiger prawns from Asia and Singapore are good. And when shopping for fresh shell-on prawns, look for the ones that are nice and plump, and smell them. I know you might not like the idea of smelling prawns in the fishmonger, but I have a rule: nothing can betray the nose of a good cook.

When prawns are getting old, they take on a pungent ammonia smell (skate and rock adopt a similar whiff) and if that's what hits you, then don't buy them. Far better to smell and say 'Oh, my gosh!' than to pay good money for something that will have to be thrown in the bin.

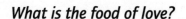

What is the food of love?

'The food of love is the food that encapsulates
and encompasses all the senses. For me, that food
is sea urchin – sensuous on the tongue, striking
to the eye, cleansing to the nose, the sound of the
ocean, an aural delight, and soft to the touch.'

—Antony Worrall Thompson

16. THE EGG BASKET

For the perfect poached egg

In a large saucepan boil about 2 litres (3½ pints) of unsalted water and 7 tbsp vinegar. Using a wooden spoon, swirl the water and let it settle to become a gentle vortex. Drop in the pre-cracked egg, and allow the egg to poach for 3 minutes.

NB: Always use the freshest eggs possible. The freshness of an egg can be identified thus: the more liquid the egg white, the older the egg.

For the perfect fried egg

In his autobiography, *The Devil in the Kitchen*, Marco Pierre White manages to teach readers how to fry an egg while simultaneously explaining his cooking philosophy.

> Let's just think for a moment about a fried egg. It's not the most inspired dish, but then again, if you can't cook an egg, what can you cook? And actually, a perfectly cooked fried egg is quite beautiful.
>
> Apply the cook's brain and visualise that fried egg on the plate. Do you want it to be burned around the edges? Do you want to see craters on the egg white? Should the yolk look as if you'd need a hammer to break into it? The answer to all three questions should be No. Yet the majority of people still crack an egg and drop it into searing hot oil or fat and

continue to cook it on high heat. You need to insert earplugs to reduce the horrific volume of the sizzle. And the result, once served up in a pool of oil, is an inedible destruction of that great ingredient – the egg. Maybe that's how you like it, in which case carry on serving your disgusting food. Meanwhile, the rest of us can think about what we really want to see on the plate. We want that egg to look beautiful and appetising because then when we eat it, we shall all be happy. We want the white to be crater-free and unblackened around its edges. The yolk should be glistening, just a thin film that can be easily pierced by a fork to let the yellowness run out. That's the picture.

How do we create it? Slowly heat a heavy-based pan on very low heat, perhaps for five minutes and once it is hot enough put in some butter, letting it gently melt. Then take your egg from a basket and crack it into a pan (I don't keep eggs in the fridge as it only lengthens the cooking process because you are dealing with a chilled ingredient.)

If the heat seems too high, remove the pan from the heat for a few seconds and let it cool down. Basically, if you can hear that egg cooking then the heat is too high. Carefully spoon the butter over the top of the egg. After about five minutes you have your magnificent fried egg – more of an egg poached in butter – just the way you had pictured it on the plate.

You crack an egg and some of the shell falls into the mixing bowl. Don't worry, don't fret and don't dip your fingers in to retrieve the piece of shell. Simply place the shell in your hand into the bowl and close to the fragment. Magnetism brings the two together, and the broken piece can be easily removed from the bowl.

How Scottish are Scotch eggs?

The Scotch egg, which is a boiled egg wrapped in forcemeat and then fried, was created in the 18th century by a cook at Fortnum and Mason, the grand store which to this day remains an institution in London's West End, and given to travellers as they set off by horse and carriage.

It was probably a 'scotched egg' before it was the Scotch egg: 'scotched' means 'crushed', which is what you do with the meat case that surrounds the egg. However, the Scottish did a good trade in eggs and transported zillions of them to London. These were preserved by being boiled, and therefore perhaps this is the origin of the name. Isabella (Mrs) Beeton's Scotch eggs are the best I've tasted. Scotch eggs are great fun to make at home with children: quite a messy yet highly rewarding culinary experience. Here is Mrs Beeton's recipe, slightly adapted.

Makes 4 Scotch Eggs

Ingredients:
4 eggs (you guessed it)

For the sausage coating:
500g (1lb 2oz) sausagemeat
2 tbsp suet
3 tbsp breadcrumbs
rind of half lemon
½ tsp mace (or to your taste)
1 egg, beaten
cayenne pepper, to your taste
salt, to your taste

Method:

1. Combine the coating ingredients.
2. Hard boil the eggs, and peel.
3. Cover the eggs in the forcemeat mixture (use wet hands to make the job easy).
4. Shallow fry (for about eight minutes in total, turning once so that the coating browns to your satisfaction). Alternatively, deep fry.

Note: The meat-covered eggs are *not* rolled in breadcrumbs before frying.

Hungry soldiers

We can stay with Scotland, for a moment. It has frequently been said that an army (that is, a successful one) marches on its stomach. That was certainly not the case when the English fought the Scots at the Battle of Flodden on 9 September 1513.

Francis Martin Norman observes in *The Battle of Flodden* (published 1908):

> In this fierce and sanguinary battle both sides fought with the utmost bravery and determination. There was one material disadvantage, however, on the side of the English which ought not to be overlooked. For two or three days previous September 9th their provisions had been scanty, and on that day they had absolutely nothing whatsoever to eat and drink, except the muddy waters of the Till and pools. Starting breakfastless, they performed those long marches – five miles in the case of the rear guard, twelve in that of the Van Guard – and, 'blackfasting as they were born', fought

a stubborn and terrible battle at the end of the day against foes who had been well housed and well fed … That was an amazing and magnificent achievement which could not fail to command the wonder and admiration of all who reflected upon it, and spoke volumes for the grit of the hardy race who performed it.

Do you like perfectly soft boiled eggs?

In which case, place your eggs into boiling water for these times:

Hen: 4 minutes
Bantam: 2 minutes, 50 seconds
Gull: 2 minutes, 10 seconds
Quail: 1 minute, 22 seconds
Ostrich: 45 minutes
Shark: 3 minutes
Turtle (where legal): raw, or 2 minutes

Ant eggs

In Thailand red ant eggs are a versatile and nutritious food whether eaten on their own or as an ingredient in recipes like Yam Kai Mot Daeng (a salad), Kaeng Kai Mot Daeng (a soup) or Kai Jiow Kai Mot (an omelette). Let's not forget Kai Mot Daeng Op, in which lightly salted ant eggs are wrapped in banana leaves and then roasted. Yummy.

In Mexico you can order escamoles. These are the larvae of ants of the genus *Liometopum*, harvested from the roots of the agave or maguey plants in Mexico (from which tequila and mezcal are made, respectively). In some forms of Mexican cuisine, escamoles are considered a delicacy and are sometimes referred to as 'insect caviar'. They have a cottage cheese-like consistency and taste buttery, yet slightly nutty. Sometimes eggs are thrown in for extra crunch.

Strange uses of egg timers

In the winter of 2012 drought was declared in south-east England at the earliest time of year on record. This prompted water companies to send out waterproof 'egg timers' to residents so they didn't linger in the shower and reduce the dwindling water stocks. The 'shower timers' gave people four minutes to wash themselves.

What is the food of love?

'I find a greatest sense of love for food that I have caught, foraged or grown. All fairly obvious, but I remember taking down a brace of pigeon, plucking them whilst warm, coating them in butter and taking such care in the gentle roasting of them, as if they were the first birds I had ever cooked, almost nervous. I felt a duty to honour the birds with only a few simple, bitter leaves and a dressing made from the roasting juices, impelled to use every last scrap of them and compelled to share them.

'As I remember it, they were delicious and the whole event romantic, intimate and personal. The pigeons were loved and in return were absolutely lovely.'

—Adam Byatt, Trinity, London

THE FOODIE

17. THE CAKE TIN

The king of cooks

Marie Antonin Carême (1784–1833) was the first great chef of modern cuisine, and deservedly known as 'the cook of kings and the king of cooks'. He was born into poverty during the French Revolution, that exhilarating moment for gastronomy: chefs who had toiled for the royals and noblemen were now 'free' to open the first restaurants and serve the masses. The young Carême earned his keep in a Parisian chophouse, and went on to open a patisserie where his creations included *pièce montées croquembouche*, that towering cake of profiteroles devoured at every French celebration. He cooked for Napoleon and came to Britain to serve the Prince Regent, later George IV. However, he hated the English fogs, found London 'sombre' and returned to France. He knew that architecture – as well as art and science – is an important part of cooking: after all, we eat first with out eyes, and architecture amounts to design and presentation. Carême's legacy remains as imposing as any of his grandest *pièces montées*.

Mary Berry's favourite cakes

1. Victoria sandwich: 'It's simple and a classic, and if it's beautifully made then it's absolutely delicious …'
2. Lemon drizzle
3. Madeira
4. Family fruit cake
5. Chocolate cake.

The chocolate myth

It's a myth that you have to use a double boiler to melt chocolate. You really don't. I think this goes back to when our mothers used that cheap Scotch Bloc chocolate flavour covering. It would split unless you heated it slowly as it was so high in sugar and low in stabilising fats. Good quality dark chocolate won't burn until it reaches a pretty high temperature so if you're just making a chocolate sauce, or melting chocolate to pour into icing or something, put it straight into a pan and over a medium heat and you'll be fine.

The reluctant cook who wrote a bestseller

Lemons were the taste of the Twenties. Two recipes that were then much used, but are now forgotten, were Lemon Roll and Lemon Whiffle from *Good Cookery*, written by W.G.R. Francillon (the 'W' stood for Winifred). This book was first published in 1920 and enjoyed regular reprints for five decades.

The whiffle recipe is included below, but first a word about Winnie's charming book. We all consider ourselves to be rushed today, but in the preface of her book she reassures her readers:

'The busy housewife who wants to feed her family economically and well, and who, at the same time, with her many duties cannot give much time to cookery, will find here what she wants.' Winnie's passion was an accidental discovery. 'I was taught to cook against my will,' writes Winnie, 'and that this training was insisted on, is one of the things for which I am most thankful.'

She was despatched by her parents to learn her craft at the Gloucester School of Domestic Science and 'from the first morning was keenly interested'. She later opened her own cookery school at her home, Harcombe House, in Uplyme, Devon. Should you wish to experience the tastes of enjoyed by our (great) grandparents then try Winnie's Lemon Whiffle.

Lemon Whiffle

1 pint boiling water, 2 whites of eggs, 6 or 8oz loaf sugar, 2 tbspn arrowroot, rinds and juice of 3 large lemons.

Soak the rinds, thinly cut, overnight in the water. Strain and boil the liquid with the sugar and lemon juice. Mix the arrowroot to a smooth cream with water and pour the boiling syrup to this. Return to the pan, re-boil. When thick, add the stiffly beaten whites. Whisk after adding stiff whites till mixture piles up. When cold, serve in custard glasses.

On buttermilk

It's often needed in recipes for pancakes and scones but on a Sunday morning while still in your PJs, buttermilk is not that easy to find. Conventional wisdom suggests adding some lemon juice to your milk to create the acidity: this is to aid the baking powder to activate and give your pancakes that fluffy texture rather than a dense Scotch pancake texture. However, lemon juice quickly curdles the milk and adds a flavour that my friend Melanie (one of Britain's finest television producers) doesn't like. Cream of tartar will do the same job. So add a teaspoonful to the flour before you add the milk and eggs and you'll have really fluffy pancakes or scones.

What is the food of love?

'Whenever I am in the company of good food, all my five senses work at full capacity. I simply love good ingredients. Smelling basil and tomatoes I am immediately transported to the time when I worked in Rome, when the most important decisions of the day always involved ingredients. The food of love would be my mother's carrot cake. It takes me back to the summers of my youth, to a carefree existence in the mountains of Switzerland. My mother always cooked her carrot cake for my birthday and even though she died when I was quite young, the light texture, the warm aroma and the delicious taste will always take me to my mother's memory.'

—Anton Mosimann, OBE

... and here is Anton Mosimann's food of love: his mother's carrot cake (also made by his grandmother), which he often serves simply dusted with icing sugar.

Makes 1 × 25cm (10in) cake

Ingredients:
2 lemons
6 eggs, separated
300g (10oz) caster sugar
300g (10oz) carrots, finely grated
300g (10oz) ground almonds
100g (3½oz) golden sultanas
80g (scant 3oz) walnuts, chopped
75g (2½oz) cornflour
pinch of ground cinnamon
2 tsp baking powder
apricot glaze
icing sugar, to dust
marzipan carrots

Filling:
250g (9oz) cream cheese
30ml (1fl oz) honey

Method:
1. Preheat the oven to 180°C (350°F/Gas Mark 4). Grease and line a 25cm (10in) cake tin.
2. Finely grate the zest from both lemons and squeeze the juice from one.
3. Beat the egg yolks in a bowl with half the caster sugar and the lemon zest and juice until pale and sticky.
4. Carefully fold in the carrots, almonds, sultanas and walnuts.

5. Sift the cornflour, cinnamon and baking powder together and fold in lightly with a spatula. Whisk the egg whites until stiff, then fold in the remaining sugar. Carefully fold this into the carrot mixture.

6. Spoon the mixture into the prepared tin and bake for 50–60 minutes. Test to see that the cake is cooked through by piercing with a skewer – if it comes out clean, it is cooked. Leave to cool, then remove from the tin.

7. Make the filling: combine the cream cheese and honey and mix well. When the cake is completely cool, cut it in half horizontally, then spread a layer of filling over the top of one half. Place the other half on top, then spread the remainder of the filling around the sides of the cake.

8. Brush the surface of the cake with warm apricot glaze and leave to set.

9. Dust with icing sugar and, if feeling adventurous, decorate with marzipan carrots.

18. THE WINDOW BOX

Medieval herbs

Herbs are tasty, vibrant and good for us. Each herb performs a role or two. Basil, for instance, aids sleep. Our medieval ancestors were obsessed with herbs, and turned to them frequently. Remember, disease and illness were common and doctors and physicians might have been a day's journey away. The subject was covered in a publication, *The Grete Herball*, in which the author felt compelled through brotherly love to show how man may be 'helped with green herbs of the garden and weeds of the fields'.

To ensure domestic harmony, mugwort was placed under the front door 'whereby man nor woman can annoy this house'. To create happiness: 'Take four leaves and four roots of verbena in wine, then sprinkle the wine all about the house where the eating is and they shall all be merry.' And wet.

> **Things that thrive in a window box:**
> Radish, spring onion, lettuce,
> mizuna, pak choi, rocket.

A tribute to coriander

Coriander is an ancient herb that has been in cultivation for at least 3,000 years. The Romans introduced it to Britain but the Romans were nothing compared to Delia Smith who, in the mid-1980s, used it in a few recipes and – hey presto! – every home cook became obsessed with the herb.

Many believe that the manna in the Old Testament is coriander seed: 'When the children of Israel were returning to their homeland from slavery in Egypt, they ate manna in the wilderness.' It is still one of the traditional bitter herbs to be eaten at Passover. Coriander (*Coriandrum sativum*) has many common names throughout the world: Chinese parsley, yuen sai, pak chee, fragrant green, dhania pattar, and so on. It is used to treat loss of appetite and is good for the digestive system. In fact, it stimulates the appetite by aiding the secretion of gastric juices.

The leaves are perfect in salads, spicy dishes, salsas and with meat, poultry and fish. The seeds can be heated or toasted – grind and use in curry pastes.

Coriander, cooking with it and the cure for colic by Manpreet Singh Ahuja

By way of introduction, Manpreet Singh Ahuja is head chef at Chor Bizarre, the well-established Indian restaurant in Mayfair. One day we met to discuss life and he veered onto the far more important issue of coriander.

Coriander is not only loved by gourmets: I'd also advise parents of babies to stock up on it. I keep the herb in my fridge, and when my one-year-old son, Sehej, is suffering from colic or indigestion, I add some coriander to boiled water, let it cool and and then give it to him. Ten minutes later my little boy is completely recovered; the crying has ceased.

For centuries coriander has been used as a genuine (rather than alcoholic) digestif, but what of it as an ingredient? I love it because it brings a cooling, refreshing quality to a dish. A lot of people in Europe find its flavour rather repulsive. But once you have become accustomed to coriander you'll wonder how you ever lived without it.

Coriander is a major ingredient in the cuisines of India, Thailand and Vietnam, and Mexicans love it in guacamole.

When I was a child growing up in India, I used to go with my grandmother to the vegetable market. At each vegetable stall, as the tomatoes, courgettes or okra were being put into her bag, my grandmother would ask the vendor, 'Can you please pop some coriander into the bag?' And that's how she ended up with free herbs.

On our walk home, I would take a few leaves of the coriander and munch away. When I started cooking, I found to my delight it was an ingredient that can be used in almost anything and everything. It does not take away – by which I mean it does not mask the flavours of other herbs – but only adds to a dish.

Coriander is part of the carrot family and is available in two forms. One is the seed of the flower. The other is the leaf. Both are very different in flavour. Seeds cannot substitute leaves and vice versa.

As far as seeds are concerned, when they are crushed they have an undertone of orange peel and lemon. Like most of the spices used in Indian cuisine, it is a slightly bitter undertone, which is lost during the cooking process. Crushed seeds will also thicken a sauce.

As far as the leaves are concerned, they are bitter and fragrant. If they are added at the beginning of cooking, the sharp flavour subsides.

Here is a very simple but delicious soup. Place chopped fresh tomatoes and coriander (including the root) in a saucepan, season with salt and pepper, cover with cold water and bring to the boil before simmering slowly. The result is a thin broth which is highly aromatic. If you want it slightly spicy then add a teaspoon of red chilli powder (or chopped green chillies). If you want to make more of a meal of it, then put in some chicken pieces and cook them with the soup.

There is also a delicious vegetarian dish, based on the *avial*, a dish that is much loved in South India and which involves steaming vegetables.

1. In a blender, mix coriander leaves, curry leaves, chickpeas and yoghurt so that you have a light green coloured paste.

2. In a saucepan, slowly cook the paste with mustard seeds, chopped red chilli, creamed coconut and more yoghurt.

3. Sauté chopped aubergines, courgette, carrots and yam and serve with the sauce, which is very light. Alternatively, cook the vegetables in the sauce.

Coriander is also lovely with fish. Combine fresh coriander, coriander seeds and desiccated coconut and use the mixture as a coating for cod. Grill the cod and serve it with the yoghurt sauce that I mentioned above (to complement the fish, you can cook onions and tomatoes in the sauce).

I make a good chutney by mixing coriander with some mint (these two herbs make a fragrant and aromatic combination), green chilli and yoghurt. It is that simple – you don't have to wait for a pickling process. Spread it on bread, or serve it with tomatoes and cheese.

I should make a couple of important points. Firstly, don't ever chop coriander before washing it. If you have bought a bunch of coriander, get it home, steep it in cold water to get rid of the dirt, drain well in a colander and then chop it. To store it, keep it in an airtight container in the fridge. But ideally, fresh coriander should be used quickly. The seeds should be kept in a dark, cool place and used within six months.

If you are cooking curries, add leaves and roots at the end to retain their fragrance. (The roots, which contain the maximum flavour and are extremely aromatic, should also be used rather than discarded.) And think of coriander as the cooling agent. Chillies, cloves, cinnamon – using too much of these ingredients will have a drastic effect on the dish. But a bit more coriander is not going to harm you. In fact, I have never come across anyone who has an allergy to coriander. What does that tell me? Whatever you do with it, coriander is safe.

Does coriander reduce flatulence?

This is true: coriander is known for sorting out flatulence – while raw onions encourage flatulence. This vulgar subject brings to mind the great wisdom of Charles Elmé Francatelli (not merely a Victorian chef but also chef to Queen Victoria, no less). I am thinking of his recipe entitled 'A simple remedy against wind on the stomach'. It is simple: 'A few drops (say four) of essence of peppermint on a lump of sugar.'

On finding snails in your window box

You must eat them. Why not?

If you enjoy snails in posh restaurants then you pay the price – they are imported from France, where they go by the more exotic name of *escargots*, and are expensive. At the time of writing, diners at La Brasserie in Chelsea can order six escargots in their shells, baked in the oven with garlic and parsley butter, and the treat will cost ten pounds and eighty pence.

There was a time in France when snails were considered a pest and young children were paid by wine producers to scour vineyards and collect the slimy hermaphrodites. Then they shot – at a surprisingly fast speed for snails – to the top of the gourmet's list. They became fashionable to eat. So much so that the Commerce of Dijon asked that the snails be considered as game – with a close season like gamey game.

In your garden, snails are free, very fresh and probably better than French snails. There's no waiter to tip.

There are some 1,600 varieties of snail around the world, but they flourish best near lime and chalk: lime forms their shell. The garden snail, *Helix aspersa*, which came to Britain with the Romans, is the one most cultivated for gourmet food and is known as petit gris. You'll find it in your garden.

You can't always eat garden snails immediately. It's best to ensure that any toxins they may have consumed are first purged from their systems. Here's what to do:

1. Wash them.
2. For the first two days, leave the snails without any food and regularly wash them.
3. On day three give them a carrot and leave them until their droppings turn orange.
4. Wash them again; place them in the fridge in a sealed container. The chill will send them into a deep slumber.

When it is time to cook them:

1. Boil a saucepan of water and add the snails. Boil for 3 minutes and drain. Allow to cool,
2. Use a cocktail stick or skewer to remove the snails from their shells.
3. Take a large frying pan and a large steak. Over a medium heat, toss a generous amount of butter and let it melt, bubble and foam. Add the steak.
4. Fry one side, turn, and fry the other.
5. Remove the steak from the pan, and place it on a warm plate.
6. Return the pan to the heat, add a large knob of butter and, once it has melted, pour in a glass of red wine and the snails. Twist the pepper mill. Let the wine evaporate and reduce in volume. Taste. Season with salt.
7. Garnish the steak with the snails, 'nap' (coat) with the sauce and eat.

Slugs: prepare in the same way as snails.

What is the food of love?

'It is what we do at Clos Maggiore with every dish. It's about giving maximum flavours in our food, seasoning, attention and care, as much as we can. We want the people to taste all the hard work and pleasure we have invested in order to cook their meal. We want them to remember it for the right reasons. It can be a fragrant San Marzano tomato salad with basil, olive oil, capers, aged balsamic vinegar with burrata. Or a slow-cooked beef short rib, which takes many hours of attention and meticulous care for robust and intense flavours. In both cases, love is about respecting the produce, great cooking and seasoning to only one goal: pleasing our guests and making them remember how food should taste. When we achieve this, this is mission accomplished. Food with no love and soul is boring and tasteless.'

—Marcellin Marc, Clos Maggiore
(voted London's Most Romantic
Restaurant, Harden's Guide 2014)

19. THE COCKTAIL SHAKER

For this chapter, the Foodie has turned to the master of cocktails, John Collingwood. A man with an incredible palate, he travels the world, going from bar to bar, training men and women to become mixologists. Over to you John … and easy on the ice.

One of the biggest mistakes that people make when trying to make their own delicious cocktail is to ignore the simple principles of balance and flavour. What you must start to do is to think of creative cocktail making as merging the art of baking a cake and making a delicious curry. It is all about mastering the classic recipe but then adapting it to your taste, and this is when the real fun begins.

When my mam taught me how to make a Victoria sponge, she gave me a sure-fire recipe that would work every time. She explained: '2oz [60g] of butter, 2oz [60g] of caster sugar, 4oz [120g] of self-raising flour, 2 eggs and ¼ teaspoon of either almond or vanilla essence (if you want to be posh!)'

What I saw in front of me was not a recipe for a wonderful cake but a gateway into explaining how to make a balanced and delightful cocktail. This is all down to what I like to call the golden ratios.

The golden ratios

If you look at the main ingredients of the Victoria sponge recipe the ratios are 4 (flour) : 2 (butter) : 2 (caster sugar). A similar principle is the same for one of the greatest cocktail families, the sour.

The sour follows the idea of using three ingredients: any spirit, citrus and sweetness. In my opinion the best ratio for these is 4:2:1. The cool thing is that it is all down to your personal preference: if you want the drink to be a little bit sweeter then go for it; all I would say is follow this ratio first and then you can easily adapt it. The key for this style of drink is to master the art of balance.

What excites me about this is the fact you can use ANY spirit; you don't have to go out and buy a whole host of new spirits, just look in your cupboard and see what you have got. A good little trick to remember is that for every bottle of alcohol you will be able to make ten cocktails, if you use 60ml (2fl oz) for each.

Now you have to check you have sufficient ice. One of the biggest mistakes people make is that they think ice is going to make their drink weaker, when it is actually the complete opposite. Ice will keep ice cold. When you use two or three ice cubes in a drink it will melt much quicker, resulting in it becoming diluted, warmer and ultimately not as palatable. Fill your glass to the brim with it and you will be amazed what a difference it will make. A wise man once told me 'It will stay stronger for longer' – and you can always make yourself another. Trust me, go out and buy a bag of ice from the corner shop or supermarket, keep it in the freezer ... it will make your life easier. Use your ice trays for other things, like blending and then freezing raspberries or strawberries when they are in season; these can then be used for a whole host of other things some of which we will touch on later.

When you are out shopping, pick up some lemons or limes. Have a think how many drinks you'll be making and, depending on how juicy they are, you will be able to make approximately one or two cocktails per fruit. If you see any delicious seasonal soft fruits then put them in the basket.

If you decide you want your drink to be long then buy some 'lengtheners'. You can be all classical and go for soda; if you want something a little bit fiery then ginger beer would be awesome, or a fruit juice will never go amiss. Just start to think what YOU want your drinks to taste like and buy what YOU want. Being creative is the fun part!

Let the good times roll

When you get home you need to get yourself organised:

1. Place your ice in the freezer, as you don't want it to melt.

2. Make yourself some home-made sugar syrup. Get a cup (approximately 8fl oz/250ml) and measure two cups of white sugar (caster or granulated) and one cup of water and put into a pan on a low heat. When the sugar has dissolved, put it to one side to cool. Once it has cooled, put it into a jug or container and place in the fridge. It will keep for about a week.

   (If you want to be creative, add in some extra flavours. Ideas could be flavoured tea bags, spices like cinnamon bark and star anise, or simply using a potato peeler to add in the zest of an orange or grapefruit. The only difference when making a flavoured syrup is that you need to bring all the ingredients to the boil first, reduce to a simmer and then allow it to bubble away for five minutes. Then remove from the heat and follow the same process explained above.)

3. Hunt out your glassware and give it a clean and polish. Tumblers will be best for short drinks and Collins or highball for long drinks.

4. Find something to accurately measure with. If you have a jigger/measurer then that is awesome but an egg cup or espresso cup will suffice.

5. Wash a lemon or lime and then cut into eight wedges and put into a bowl.

6. Squeeze a few lemons or limes and place the juice into a small pouring jug.

Now you are all prepped and ready to go.

Sour

1. Get a tumbler.
2. Measure 1 part or ½fl oz/15ml sugar syrup and 2 parts or 1fl oz/30ml lemon or lime juice into your glass. Give it a taste and if you want to add more sweetness, add in ½ teaspoon at time.
3. Measure 4 parts or 2fl oz/60ml of your spirit into the glass.
4. Top with ice, give it a stir and garnish with either a wedge of either lemon or lime.

Berry sour

All you need to do is to place 8–10 raspberries or a few strawberries into the base of your glass and gently press with a flat-ended rolling pin (or use a frozen berry ice cube from your freezer). Then repeat the process shown above.

Collins

Quite simply this cocktail is a sour that is served long and traditionally topped with soda. Therefore all you do is replace the tumbler
glass with a highball or Collins. Follow the same method and then
lengthen it with your mixer of choice.

As you can see, I have not mentioned any spirits to use, as I want
you to get creative – as to me that is what making drinks should all
be about: having fun and enjoying them with friends and family.

20. THE TRUFFLE DRAWER

....

Quite an interesting chapter, even if you are not rich enough to buy truffles ... you can find them for free in England.

On the subject of truffles

The truffle is edible black fungus which takes its name from the Latin for 'lump' (and you'll know why when you see one). Gourmets divide truffles by their colours. The south-west of France claims the credit for producing the finest black truffles. The north-east of Italy boasts the finest white truffles. Truffles are ridiculously expensive (white more so than black) and fools have been known to pay £150,000 for truffles that weigh about 1.5kg (3lb 5oz). Brillat-Savarin noted that 'one of the great values of truffles is their dearness; perhaps they would be less highly esteemed if they were cheaper.'

Ironically, this costly food item often tastes best when it is paired with one of the cheapest – the egg. Store a truffle with eggs and the strong scent of the funghi will permeate the egg shells and flavour the final egg dish. Equally, simple egg pasta is *bellissima* when white truffle is grated on to it. When I am rich enough I intend to buy a truffle and try Auguste Escoffier's recipe: 'When making scrambled eggs, place truffle on a fork and stir it within the eggs as they cook.'

When it comes to truffles, France and Italy have received so much attention over the past couple of centuries that it is dull. Let's swing the spotlight away from them, and look at truffles elsewhere.

The Great English Truffle Correspondence, and the master forager Eli Collins

In December 1938 *The Times* ran an article headlined 'Truffles to Seek: A Subterranean Harvest'. This prompted that prince of connoisseurs, André Simon, to write to the newspaper, saying that he had never tasted English truffles. Simon's published letter, in turn, produced bulging bags of mail from readers who were passionate about English truffles, and had fond memories of eating them.

These letters to *The Times*, and to Simon, provide one of the most enjoyable and compelling examples of epicurean correspondence. They are enlightening, highly informative and bring well-deserved recognition to a man called Eli Collins, a poodle-loving truffler from the village of Winterslow in Wiltshire.

So let's go back to the late 1930s. Pretend to be a reader of *The Times*, and adopt a posh voice …

From Lieutenant-Colonel The Hon. Ben Bathurst

[In my youth] My father engaged the services of a professional truffle hunter and his dogs to find out whether truffles grew in the woods of Cirencester Park, where there are many beech trees. Some truffles were certainly found, but in no great quantity …

It looks as though truffles require a soil with plenty of chalk or lime, and as they are found under thorn trees in the open, as well as under beech trees, it might well be argued that the tubers also require some shade …

From Mr C.J. Daun

Referring to your letter … It may interest you to know that although I had never heard of truffles in Richmond Park, I have many times heard my mother (who was born in 1823) say she had seen what she called 'truffle-dogs' hunting for truffles under the trees (I think elms) on Tooting Bec Common, but I cannot remember if she actually saw any found.

From General S.R. Wason

… I was one of Mr. Eli Collins' customers and he was supposed the best English truffle hunter … I used to buy truffles from him for Christmas presents. I paid him 5s. a pound (I am almost sure of this). Their size, as sent to me, varied from that of a walnut to a medium or small Cox's Orange Pippin. The smaller ones, I think, he gave to his dog. They were, I think, rather greyer than the French truffle as I know it, but I am not certain that I have ever eaten a fresh French truffle, and this might account for the difference in colour. I always thought we used to eat them merely boiled and with butter. One used to have to cut off their hard, rough skin, which was not an easy operation when they were hot. But having sent some to a lady, and hearing she had them *fried*, I asked my aunt Mrs Robert Norman (since died) for a recipe for cooking them, and with those I sent at Christmas 1913, I sent a copy of it. I am certain that they were finished off by being simmered in stock, according to this recipe.

After the war, I wrote again to Eli Collins (Winterslow). He was either dead or out of business, but a son or a nephew came to see me, and having given up digging truffles wanted to sell me hurdles.

From Lieut-Col. J. Bennet-Stanford

Many years ago there used to be a truffle hunter named Eli Collins who lived at Winterslow on the plain. From him I got many a pound. He had a son who carried on this profession until he got so bad with rheumatism that he could not walk. I believe he is still alive.

They both used to hunt truffles with little, white French poodles, but I believe any dog can be trained to catch them. I know of many spots where I could get a good many in five minutes if we only had trained dogs.

'*En serviette*' with butter, pepper and salt, they are delicious, but they are rather browner in colour than truffles de Périgord.

From Catherine Lady Headley

I have both seen and eaten English truffles. They were found near Amesbury by dogs brought from Winterslow. They tasted like other black truffles and were quite small and irregular, varying from the size of a marble to rather larger than a golf ball. They were found in beech plantations now owned by Colonel Bailey, Lake House, Salisbury.

A quick update: In the early 1990s Lake House, which lies in the Woodford Valley (close to Stonehenge) was bought by musician Sting and his actress wife Trudie Styler. Sting recorded his album Ten Summoner's Tales *in the house, and the couple run a 165-acre organic farm on the estate. The farm is divided into two sections: around the old Jacobean house are the permanent old pastures, the apple orchards and the milking barn. Up on the Top Land, where buzzards and curlews wheel in the thermal updrafts, the lie of the land is very different, free-draining chalk downland. In 1999 Styler co-wrote* The Lake House Cookbook *with her chef, Joe Sponzo.*

From Mrs Blanche E. Dutton

When, as a young bride, I came to my husband's home, Hinton Ampner House, Alresford, in 1888, there was an old man living in the nearby village of Cheriton who possessed a truffle-dog, which used to find truffles under the beech trees in Tichborne Park, adjoining Cheriton village. The old man used to call upon us, bringing a red handkerchief filled with glorious truffles. Some were not much bigger than large marbles, others larger than golf balls. We had them well boiled and served hot in a napkin. When they came to table they were quite black outside and knobbly. This knobbly crust we pared away, revealing a delicate-coloured, greyish-pink, firm flesh inside. We ate them with butter and they had a wonderful nutty flavour ...

We used sometimes to send our truffles to my father, who had lived much in France in his youth. He told me that he knew a shop in Paris where they sold Cheriton truffles.

From Mrs La Terrière [surely an alias]

... I have myself found some in this district (Oxon) by hand, just groping around the mould. Thin shoes will often enable one to find them on a lawn under ilex or beech trees ... Boiled and eaten hot, with butter, they are food for the Gods.

From Colonel H.G. Kennard

... About a year ago I happened to listen to a broadcast by a truffle-hunter. He was asked which was the biggest one he had ever found. He replied ... that it was one of some 4oz. on the Crawley Court estate in Hampshire. This was my old home to which my father moved when we left Wiltshire in 1878. I can't boast to having eaten English truffles myself, as I suppose we children were not deemed capable of appreciating such luxuries, but I'm pretty sure that English truffles are still found and eaten.

They are indeed.

A note about Eli Collins

The Collins family were at the centre of the truffle trade for 200 years. Eli Collins began truffle hunting at the age of nine, in the early 19th century. In his quest for the fungus, he covered eight counties. The last Collins truffler was Eli's son, Alfred. As the correspondence (above) reveals, Alfred's ill-health prevented him from continuing this seemingly lucrative career. They could bring home 25lb (11kg) of truffles on their best days and on one occasion Eli's dogs found a truffle weighing more than 2lb (900g), which he presented to the then Prince of Wales, later King Edward VII. The prince insisted on paying for the truffle with a 'photograph' of his mother, Queen Victoria, and a gold sovereign.

Truffle wisdom

Leave truffles in risotto rice to infuse. Better still, place truffle in a box with eggs to allow the aroma to permeate the shell.

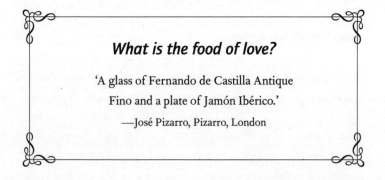

What is the food of love?

'A glass of Fernando de Castilla Antique
Fino and a plate of Jamón Ibérico.'

—José Pizarro, Pizarro, London

21. THE (COCO)NUT BOWL

Worshipping the coconut
by Manish Mehrotra

By way of introduction, Manish Mehrotra is an Indian chef who has won many awards. His restaurants have included Tamarai in London. He spoke to me with great passion on one particular subject: the coconut. He talked and talked, and thankfully I recorded his delicious monologue on the nut. Settle back and enjoy, as Manish goes coconuts ...

When I was little I worshipped the coconut. Quite literally worshipped it. I grew up in Bihar, in the northern part of India, where the coconut is not a common crop and therefore is not hugely popular. But once a year we celebrated a particular religious festival that involved my family decorating a coconut so that it represented a goddess. The shell would be wrapped in red cloth and placed on a font, and then we would kneel in front of the coconut and pray.

These prayers would last, intermittently of course, for ten days. The festival ended with the ceremonial cracking open of the coconut. We would all be given a bit to eat and I savoured every mouthful of the delicious white flesh. I have a vivid memory of being caught as I tried to make off with the coconut before the festival had finished. I got a real shouting-at from my parents, so I didn't do that again.

Then I grew up and became a chef, and found myself cooking Thai cuisine, which has coconut as one of its major ingredients.

And my wife, Vindhya, comes from the southern part of India where coconut features heavily in the diet, so she encouraged me to cook with it.

There you have it. Coconut may have been a rare treat in my childhood, but now it is in my house and in my restaurant, Tamarai, every day of the year. Starters, main courses and desserts benefit from this wonderful ingredient that is available through every season.

It goes well with everything. In fact, I was surprised to discover that coconut milk is quite delicious when it is used as a Thai soup (flavoured with ginger) poured on to pan-fried foie gras. It might sound like an odd combination – and I have never seen it anywhere else – but my customers love it.

For vegetarians, there is a delicious dish of croquettes made from tofu and coconut. I use coconut milk powder to mask the odour of tofu, which is not particularly appetising. The tofu is crushed overnight to remove the water content. Then the powder, along with lemongrass and coriander, are incorporated, as well as Thai sweet chilli sauce, which has been reduced so that it has a syrup consistency. Small balls are made from the mixture and they are coated in breadcrumbs and deep-fried. Impressed customers have said to me, 'From this day on, I will see tofu differently.'

When shopping for coconuts, you need to pick up the fruit, give it a shake and feel the weight of it. It must feel nice and heavy and you'll be able to hear a nice amount of water inside. If you spot any signs of leakage don't buy it.

Many people break the shell by wrapping the coconut in a tea towel and giving it a good whack with a hammer. That method can be messy and leave you with dozens of fragments of shell on the flesh.

There is another way, but it requires skill. Holding the coconut in one hand, rotate it and tap it gently with the blunt side of a large knife blade. Now that the shell is weakened, give it a slightly harder hit in the centre. The shell should – I say should – split in half.

If the flesh smells rancid (and it won't if you have followed my shopping advice) don't even attempt to eat it.

If you want to make coconut milk, soak the pulp in warm water for half an hour. Then pulverise it and strain the milk through a muslin cloth.

How healthy is it? Well, it contains a high amount of saturated fat but there is a theory that this fat is healthier than the saturated fat found in other products. All I can say is that I have been to Thailand and South India where coconut is a popular part of the diet and I haven't seen too many fat people suffering from heart disease. This nut is also rich in zinc, iron, calcium and protein and has less sugar content than, say, apples and oranges.

Every part of the coconut and its palm can be used in some form or another. The palm tree is used to make huts and houses; the leaves make brooms; the coir (those fibres on the husk) are used for mattresses and carpets. Then you have the coconut water to drink, the flesh to eat, the shell becomes a vessel for food or drink and the oil is a hair conditioner. In Malay the tree is known as 'the tree of a thousand uses'. Nothing, but nothing, is thrown away.

Manish's lamb shanks in Malay curry (with coconut milk as a star ingredient)

1. Put fresh herbs like lemongrass, Thai ginger and lime leaves into coconut milk, and add a touch of fish sauce and sugar.
2. Immerse the lamb shanks in the milk mixture and cook in the oven at 160°C (320°F/Gas 3) for about 2½ hours.
3. Remove from the oven, strain the coconut milk mixture and add to it curry powder and chopped tomato.

4. Allow the mixture to simmer for 20 minutes before returning the shanks to it.
5. Finally, serve with chopped basil.

It really is yummy: the coconut flavour is totally absorbed by the meat; the lamb will melt in your mouth.

What is the food of love?

'The food of love is blueberry pancakes with maple syrup on a Saturday morning. The food of love is anything cooked for friends and family. The food of love is truffle honey.

'And then … and then there is the love of food. The love of food is discussing what you are going to be having for lunch over breakfast. The love of food is waking up in the night, writing down recipes conjured up in your dreams. It is the sound of the smacking lips of your five- and two-year-olds as they wordlessly devour something new for the first time. The love of food is the appreciative silence that washes over a table of people as they taste the first bite of a meal you have cooked for them.'

—Dhruv Baker, *MasterChef* winner, 2010

THE FOODIE

22. THE CHEESE BOARD

'A dessert without cheese is like a beautiful
woman who has lost an eye.'

—Jean Anthelme Brillat-Savarin

Cheese gifts

Cheese is a thoughtful gift to take to Sunday lunch, but sometimes it is not well received. When Queen Victoria married Prince Albert in 1840 the couple were presented with a gigantic wheel of cheddar. One of the largest cheddars ever made, it weighed half a tonne (1,110lb), and was nine feet in diameter. As the Queen was four feet and eleven inches tall, she was looking at a cheese slice that was about twice her height.

It is said that she was puzzled, embarrassed and possibly offended, and therefore relieved when the cheese-makers asked if they might borrow the wheel to take it on a tour of Britain, showing it off. A kind of cheese gig, if you like. So off it went, around the country, and when it came back it was grubby and scruffy as lots of people had touched it in the same way a modern-day rock star is groped by groupies.

The Palace said, 'We don't want it now.'

The cheese producers said, 'We don't want it either.'

And so this stinking great slab of cheddar was passed on to the Chancery. What happened to it next remains to this day a mystery.

US presidents also receive cheese gifts. In 1801 Thomas Jefferson received a Cheshire cheese weighing 1,200lb, and in the

1830s New York cheddar producers presented a giant cheddar to Andrew Jackson. This one weighed three-quarters of a ton and, as with Queen Victoria's gift, no one quite knew what to do with it. Jackson's cheese spent about two years in a vestibule at the White House until some bright spark came up with an idea: when George Washington's birthday was celebrated, Jackson threw open the doors of the White House to the entire city, and the cheese was shared among the inhabitants. According to witnesses, 'the whole area was infected with cheese.' It was eaten within two hours, just a morsel or two being saved for the president.

Why can you eat mould in blue cheese and not on bread?

Some moulds produce toxins that can cause a variety of health problems, but many are perfectly harmless. If you eat mouldy bread you have no idea which moulds are growing on it.

Blue cheese, however, is made with specific strains of moulds which are deliberately introduced to ripen the cheese and give it flavour. These strains are food grade and have been used for hundreds of years. We know that they do not produce toxins and the manufacturers are very rigorous over their quality control so that they only introduce the correct strains.

The world's most expensive cheese

It costs about £300 per pound (450g), and is not even French!

Christer and Ulla Johansson started the 59-acre 'Moose House' in the late 1990s in Bjursholm, some 400 miles north of Stockholm. Moose House has fourteen moose in the fields, but only three of them – Gullan, Haelga and Juna – can be milked.

The animals were found as abandoned calves in the woods and were taken in by the Johansson family. The domesticated moose stay outdoors all year and weigh about 500kg (1,100lb) each.

Moose cheese is extremely costly because it is produced in very small quantities only between May and September. It takes up to two hours to milk a moose, with each producing up to a gallon of milk per day. Compared to cow's milk, moose milk is higher in butterfat and solids while boasting elevated levels of aluminium, iron, selenium, and zinc. Moose milk contains 12 per cent fat and 12 per cent protein.

It is kept refrigerated and curdling is done three times per year – yielding 660 pounds (300kg) of cheese per year. Made in three varieties, the moose cheese can be sampled only at the farm's restaurant and a few upscale Swedish hotels and restaurants.

Can cheese be frozen?

It kind of takes the romance out of it but yes, you can freeze cheese for up to two months with pretty much no ill effects. Wrap in wax paper, then in foil and into plastic and you're laughing. This is great if you like to have a good cheese board when entertaining but hate the waste afterwards. Allow the cheese to defrost for three or four hours, depending on its size.

One of the smelliest cheeses

Epoisses is not as old or renowned as Roquefort; but it can boast a legitimate claim to the smelliest cheese crown, thanks in part to two distinguished fans: Jean Anthelme Brillat-Savarin, the influential 18th-century gastronome, and Napoleon Bonaparte, the late emperor-king of just about everything.

It was Brillat-Savarin, philosopher-gourmand, who dubbed Epoisses the king of cheeses – a declaration not to be dismissed, considering the seriousness with which he regarded cheese.

If you have the chance to taste some ripe, runny Epoisses, you might be surprised by its powerful odour, which has proven offensive to many. There are even rumours that it was banned on public transportation in France. Napoleon had his peculiarities, but how, you might ask, could a sophisticated connoisseur like Savarin love a cheese that smelled to heaven? Well, legend has it that his culinary aesthetic was so enlarged, so distinguished, that he would carry dead birds around in his pockets so that he could savour the aroma.

In 1991 the cheese was awarded AOC status, which states that the manufacture must follow the following rules: the milk's coagulation must be performed by lactic acid and continue for sixteen hours. The curd must be cut roughly as opposed to being broken. After drainage, only dry salt may be used.

Under AOC regulation the cheese may only be made in listed communes in the Côte-d'Or, Haute-Marne, and Yonne departments.

What is the food of love?

'When I think of the food of love, I think of my mother
and how her passion for taste inspired me from a very
young age. Many of my dishes now relate to childhood
memories. As a toddler I remember her making the best
creamy mash with grated smoked ham; it was simple yet
full of flavour. Another childhood favourite of mine as
I grew older was *Poulet Landais*. She would rub a piece
of baguette with a garlic clove and then stuff it into the
chicken. The bread would soak up all the flavours of the
chicken, including the garlic and herbs, and she would let
me eat it, straight from the oven. It was utterly delicious!

'A wonderful family memory was our annual
trip to a hunting lodge and we would all dive
into a large terracotta pot filled with slow-cooked
sweetbreads, mushrooms and Madeira wine. My
mother inspired my love of food, undoubtedly.'

—Eric Chavot, Brasserie Chavot, London

EPILOGUE

....

Let us leave the washing up until the morning

Farewell dear reader. It's been a feast of unimaginable fun, hasn't it? Well, I've enjoyed it. Are you feeling full, or still famished? If we were in the Balkans I would now be throwing water in your direction. It's an ancient tradition – when guests leave your home you chuck water behind their feet. The notion is a considerate one: as the water's course is smooth and easy, so may the traveller's path be.

Oh no, where's my jug gone?

Instead, let me leave you with an enchanting tale that represents the food of love. You'll have heard, of course, of 'a flitch of bacon'.

In the 1300s a flitch was a 'side' of meat, usually bacon. In those days, in certain parts of England, a flitch was awarded to married couples. Not just any old, boring married husband and wife. These ones had to have been married for one year and one day. There was a ceremony, the couple was asked a few questions, swore a pledge and then off they went, carrying their flitch, trumpets playing.

The flitch ceremony was not a common event, but certainly took place at a few grand estates, the side of pig being a gift from the landowner. The manor of Wychnor Hall in Staffordshire was granted to Sir Philip de Somerville in 1336 from the Earl of Lancaster for a small fee but also on condition that he kept ready 'at all times of the year but Lent, one bacon-flitch hanging in his hall at Wychnor, to be given to every man or woman who demanded it a year and a day after the marriage, upon their swearing they would not have changed for none other'. The couple were required to produce two chums to confirm that the oath was true.

If you have been married for a year and a day you can try the oath at home. It reads (and I've modernised the English a little):

'Hear ye, maintainer and giver of this Bacon, that I, [husband's name], sayeth I wedded [wife's name], my wife, and sayeth I had her in my keeping and at will by a year and a day after our marriage, I would not have changed for none other, fairer nor fouler, richer nor poorer, nor for none other descended of greater lineage, sleeping nor waking, at no time; and if the said [name of wife] were single, and I single, I would take her to be my wife before all the women of the world, of what conditions soever they be, good or evil, as help me God, and his saints, and this flesh, and all fleshes.'

May I be the first to congratulate you! Award yourself a flitch of bacon.

If you are a pica sufferer, you can now eat this book.

THE END

ACKNOWLEDGEMENTS

It's not quite farewell, after all.

Close your eyes and imagine that we are together celebrating the completion of this peculiar little book. All right, now open them so that you can continue reading.

The Foodie would be purposeless without you, the reader. You have given your valuable time – and perhaps even gulped painkillers – to endure the preceding pages. We might not know each other very well, but you are the reader and deserve thanks. So I raise a glass to you and with the utmost sincerity deliver this toast:

Thank you (please insert your name)

I am indebted to Duncan Heath, Editorial Director of Icon Books. Duncan and I met in May 2013 to discuss this project over coffee and Danish pastries at the St Georges Hotel, near BBC HQ in London W1. Quick deviation, but why do we call them *Danish* pastries? The Danish can't take all the credit for them. In fact, the Danish bakers went on strike in the 1850s and the gifted Viennese bakers and confectioners left Austria and went to Denmark to fill the vacant jobs. They took their own recipes, one of which became known by the Danish as 'Vienna bread'. Add a bit more egg to the recipe and you have the pastry we now know as Danish. It doesn't seem fair.

Anyway, Duncan, it has been a pleasure to work with you and your team at Icon. I presented my editor, Robert Sharman, with a manuscript of such gobbledegook and insanity that to most eyes it would have required a straitjacket. Instead, Rob gently helped me to take it to a far better place. Sure, some of the madness remains but not enough to have me locked away. Dear Rob, thank you so much.

David Wardle is the thoughtful and talented designer of *The Foodie* and Mark Ecob of its previous incarnation as *The Kitchen Magpie*. Marie Doherty (typesetter) and Sara Bryant (proofreader) are owed more than a drink, too. Meanwhile, in his former role as Publicity Director at Icon, that fine cook and connoisseur Henry Lord worked tirelessly to raise awareness of the book. I am grateful to Kiera Jamison, Kate Hewson and Nira Begum and the team at Icon.

Throughout my life I have been drawn to people who love food. They tend to be generous, warm-spirited folk who are immensely entertaining. Even those chefs with behavioural issues are still a good laugh most of the time. People who enjoy food are lovely people and I am privileged to know many chefs and cooks whose advice has been invaluable.

Adam Byatt, chef-proprietor at Trinity in Clapham, southwest London, was a supporter right from the start. Adam, your guidance and friendship has been greatly appreciated. Marco Pierre White and Raymond Blanc have also given me food, advice and cookery lessons – all of it free – and I thank them both accordingly. Romina Kennedy, please will you cook for me so that I can say thank you for both the fantastic meal and your help? Paul Donnelley, a good friend and the man with the encyclopaedic memory, should receive a case or two from someone or other.

Thank you so much to Matthew Fort, my favourite food writer, for agreeing to write about good manners. It is an honour to have your work within these pages.

It has been a privilege to work with Professor Bob Rastall, head of Food and Nutritional Sciences at the University of Reading, and his colleague Lisa Methven.

There are many other cooks and chefs whose knowledge and passion has helped to make a feast of the *Foodie*. I admire them all and thank them for their contributions. They include: Jason Atherton, Dhruv Baker, Mary Berry, Antonio Carluccio OBE, Kai Chase, Eric Chavot, Paul Hollywood, Ken Hom, Pierre Koffmann, Francesco Mazzei, James Martin, Manish Mehrotra, Anton Mosimann OBE, Roger Pizey, José Pizarro, Pascal Proyart, Michel Roux OBE, Michel Roux Junior, Manpreet Singh Ahuja, Marcus Wareing and Antony Worrall Thompson.

Hot 'Doug' Sohn, thank you for your adoring ode to hot dogs. John Collingwood, the senior drinks consultant of Fling Bar Services, you were kind to share your knowledge with the Foodie's readers. John, we all love you. Hic!

Richard Siddle, editor of *Harper's Wine & Spirit*, and Phil Connor, exceptional wine tutor, provided vinous knowledge. Melanie Jappy, the esteemed TV producer and director, shared gems of culinary wisdom.

Mo Joslin and the 17th-century historian Andrea Zuvich were incredibly helpful with food history. Jennifer Wood and all at Canton Tea Co. supplied fascinating material for the 'Teapot' chapter.

Others who deserve praise and acknowledgement for their help include: Peter Berry, Charlotte Carlisle, Shelley-Anne Claircourt, Craig and Sarah Cooper (and Sarah's Facebook friends), Fletcher Dhew, Paula Fitzherbert, Victoria Giglio, Carlo Grossi and Gemma Adams of Grossi Wines, Jessica Gunn, Chris Hutchins, Abby Kaverne at Tregothnan, Leah Kirkland, Gulli Kristmundsson, Rebecca Longhurst, Jo MacSween, Tom Magnuson, Mme Celia Martin, Dominic Midgley, Hannah Norris, Luke Prentice, Helena Riches, Sue Richmond, lovesweetpotatoes. com, Giles Sequeira, Lydia Shevell, Edwina Simon, Donald Sloan,

David Steen, Gina Steen, Tony Swatland, Chris Terry, Louise Townsend, Lee Whitlock, James Wong.

William Sitwell was thoughtful. I began the book eating Jelly Belly beans – and thank you to Victoria Reeves who supplied me with lots of interesting info about the beans (there are 16 billion beans produced per year): I'm saving it for *The Foodie 2*. In the final stages of writing, Megan Roberts kept me energised with Hotel Chocolat. I've never gone hungry!

I am grateful to the many sources of information and to the gourmets and writers who have encouraged my love of food. They include (the much-maligned) Isabella Beeton, Elizabeth David, Keith Floyd, André Simon, Giles MacDonogh and Paul Levy.

Should you wish to share your food stories, please contact me on Twitter: @jamessteen100